A BEGINNER'S GUIDE TO HEALTHY AND HAPPY RELATIONSHIPS

UNLOCK YOUR COUPLE'S POTENTIAL THROUGH COMMUNICATION, TRUST, EFFECTIVE CONFLICT RESOLUTION, AND EMOTIONAL INTIMACY

JULIA RAY

CONTENTS

INTRODUCTION

"The meeting of two personalities is like the contact of two chemical substances: if there is any reaction, both are transformed."

— CARL JUNG

In an overcrowded café, I found myself staring across the table at the person I had decided to spend my life with. You'd think that by now, after years of being together, conversation would flow like a well-rehearsed song. But that day, silence had settled between us like an unwanted guest. Our eyes met, but our souls felt miles apart. That moment slapped me awake, making me realize that love alone wasn't enough to fuel a lifetime journey with someone. If you've ever found yourself in a similar situation, feeling isolated despite being in a room full of people, or worse, feeling distant from the one person who should be your sanctuary, you know how it feels.

Navigating the intricacies of love and commitment isn't for the faint of heart. Perhaps you've discovered that already. It's like trying to solve a puzzle without seeing the bigger picture. You keep arranging and rearranging the pieces, hoping they'll magically form a beautiful image. Often the result is frustration, dissatisfaction, and a lingering feeling that something's missing.

You might be asking, "Why do relationships have to be so complicated?" That's because they involve two unique individuals trying to blend their worlds together. It's not a one-size-fits-all deal. The Harvard study on happiness wasn't kidding when it declared that the quality of our relationships significantly influences our well-being. If that's the case, why do we often find ourselves ill-equipped to handle the very thing that's supposed to make us happy?

The stark reality is that we're often thrown into relationships without a guidebook or roadmap. Society and culture have fed us romanticized versions of love, making us ill-prepared for the day-to-day grind that comes with sustaining a meaningful connection. We learn through trial and error, and sadly, many of us accumulate emotional battle scars before we even get a chance to experience what love could truly offer.

Maintaining a healthy, fulfilling relationship can be both an art and a science. But how do you even start?

Enter the **RELATE framework**—a comprehensive guide to building and sustaining love that stands the test of time. Reflect on your relationship, engage in effective communication, love passionately, address the issues, build trust, and evolve together. You're not just applying Band-Aids to your relationship woes;

you're undergoing a transformative journey that aims to enrich not just your love life but your entire existence.

The RELATE framework is not your typical relationship advice. It's a holistic, balanced, and actionable approach that respects your individuality while focusing on mutual growth. This isn't about quick fixes; it's about long-term solutions.

Let's dive in, shall we? No fluff, no unrealistic promises, just practical wisdom to guide you toward a love life worth living.

The first promise this book offers is a shift in perspective. You'll start seeing your relationship not as a minefield of problems but as a garden of possibilities. We'll tackle communication, trust, intimacy, and, yes, even the ever-elusive concept of happiness.

Can you imagine waking up next to your partner and feeling a rush of joy simply because they're there beside you? How about sitting across from them at dinner and seeing not just the food on the table but a lifetime of shared dreams, mutual respect, and undying love? This book aims to take you there. It's not a utopian dream but a reachable reality.

So, if you're tired of feeling like your relationship is running on autopilot, then this is your wake-up call. Your catalyst. This book is not offering a magic pill; it's offering a toolbox that could transform your relationship from mundane to magical, from frustrating to fulfilling.

R - REFLECT ON YOUR RELATIONSHIP

"The first step toward change is awareness. The second step is acceptance."

— NATHANIEL BRANDEN

So, what's your story? Have you ever felt this electric charge with your partner? Or perhaps your connection was more like a slow burn, gradually warming up over time. Either way, these are the sensations that often kickstart relationships. But relationships require more than just initial attraction to last. They need constant reflection and self-awareness, the cornerstone of any long-term partnership.

You see, despite the world trying to convince us that love is all about grand gestures and fairytale endings, the truth is much more nuanced. Love, in its most enduring form, thrives on self-awareness and the ability to assess your relationship honestly.

That's what we're going to focus on in this chapter: the "R" in the RELATE framework—Reflect on Your Relationship.

You might be surprised to learn that 64% of Americans claim they are very happy in their relationships. Yes, you read that correctly—64%. It sounds like a dream statistic until you realize that not all of these relationships are as picture-perfect as they appear.

We all have our own stories and experiences that shape our perception of happiness and contentment. However, true happiness in a relationship isn't just about counting your blessings; it's about recognizing your challenges and facing them head-on. It's about identifying what you need, what your partner needs, and how those needs align—or don't.

If you're nodding along, you're already ahead of the game. Realizing that there's room for reflection means you're willing to invest in your relationship's future. But how do you actually go about reflecting on your relationship?

Firstly, think about your own needs and desires. What makes you feel loved? What makes you feel secure? These aren't questions to gloss over. Spend time pondering them, maybe even jot them down. The aim isn't to judge yourself but to understand your emotional and physical triggers. Self-awareness is the first step in making any relationship work.

Now, once you're clear on what you need, it's time to turn the mirror onto your relationship. What are its strengths? What are the areas that could use some TLC? Are you both good at communicating but struggle with maintaining intimacy? Or perhaps trust is your strong suit, but you find it hard to manage conflicts effectively?

Such assessments aren't about highlighting failures; they're about illuminating pathways for growth. But this isn't a one-person show. While doing your internal audit, remember that your partner needs to be in the loop.

And let's address the elephant in the room—communication. Yes, I know the phrase "communication is key" has been thrown around so much that it's lost its impact. But let's not dismiss it entirely. Effective communication isn't just about talking; it's about listening. It's about hearing what isn't said as much as what is.

Let's not forget about intimacy, either. Many people assume that intimacy is solely about physical closeness when it's so much more. Emotional intimacy is the bedrock of any lasting relationship. It's the glue that holds everything together when the world outside is falling apart. So ask yourself, how emotionally connected do you feel to your partner?

You'll notice that we haven't touched much on conflict resolution yet, and there's a reason for that. Conflicts, as uncomfortable as they are, offer opportunities for growth. They bring underlying issues to the forefront and demand resolution. But conflicts can't be resolved without the elements we've discussed: self-awareness, honest relationship assessment, effective communication, and emotional intimacy.

The reflection doesn't end here; it's an ongoing process. It evolves as you and your relationship evolve. Because the fact is, you're not the same person you were a year ago, and neither is your partner. And that's a good thing. Change is inevitable, but growth is intentional.

So, why bother with all this reflection? Because the alternative is to drift along, allowing problems to multiply until they become insurmountable. Because taking the time to reflect on your relationship means you're investing in its longevity.

What fuels you? It's a question worth reflecting on.

Common Relationship Myths: What's Tripping You Up

"The greatest deception men suffer is from their own opinions."

— LEONARDO DA VINCI

I remember sitting in a quaint little café, a vintage porcelain teacup warming my palms as the aroma of Earl Grey wafted into the air. A friend of mine, Sarah, was across the table from me, her eyes lost in the intricate swirls of her cappuccino. We were talking about relationships, a subject that often evokes mixed emotions. Sarah was frustrated, convinced that her relationship had to fit a specific mold to be considered successful. This got me thinking: so many of us are tangled in these myths about what relationships "should" look like, and it's about time we set the record straight.

You see, these myths act like invisible puppeteers, pulling strings and steering us away from what could be a genuinely fulfilling connection with our partners. They can be so ingrained in us that we don't even realize we're buying into them.

The Myth: "Opposites Attract"

Ah, the allure of the mysterious, the unknown. There's some truth to the idea that differences can spice up a relationship. However, the key issue here is compatibility. When the initial thrill of the unknown fades away, shared values and goals become the glue that holds a relationship together. So, while opposites might attract initially, long-term success often depends on what you have in common.

The Myth: "Happy Wife, Happy Life"

This phrase has been parroted so much that it's practically a mantra. But let's be real: it misses the mark. Happiness isn't a one-person job; it's a collaborative effort. Holding onto this notion is like saying only one person in the relationship deserves to be happy, which is just absurd.

The Myth: "Never Go to Bed Angry"

It's unrealistic to think you can neatly resolve all disputes before hitting the sack. Sometimes, you need to sleep on it, get some perspective, and tackle the issue when you're both not emotionally charged. Pressuring yourself to resolve conflicts on a tight deadline can lead to rushed, insincere resolutions.

The Myth: "You Should Be Each Other's Everything"

Expecting one person to be your lover, therapist, career advisor, and exercise buddy is a surefire way to set yourself up for disappointment. It's also a colossal weight to put on someone's shoulders. Maintaining separate interests and friendships enriches your life and gives you more to bring back to the relationship.

The Myth: "Love Conquers All"

Love is potent, but let's not kid ourselves: love alone won't magically resolve financial disagreements, trust issues, or conflicting life goals. A successful relationship involves teamwork, compromise, and a lot of unsexy but essential day-to-day maintenance.

The Myth: "Communication Is Key"

Yes, communication is essential, but this cliché misses the nuance. It's not just about talking; it's about understanding. It's about recognizing when to speak, when to listen, and how to do both in a way that makes both parties feel heard and valued.

The Myth: "All You Need Is Love"

The Beatles might have been onto something, but they left out the fine print. Love is a critical ingredient, yes, but a relationship needs more. It needs mutual respect, shared experiences, and compatible life goals to thrive.

The Myth: "Just Be Yourself"

While authenticity is crucial, this advice often fails to consider that growth and change are natural parts of life and relationships. Being yourself doesn't mean refusing to evolve or adapt, especially in ways that can strengthen your relationship.

The Myth: "You Should Always Put Your Partner First"

Fulfilling relationships require you to balance self-care with caring for your partner. If you always put your partner first, you run the risk of losing yourself in the relationship, which is unhealthy for both of you.

It's not easy to cast aside these myths, especially when they've been ingrained in us through movies, books, and societal expectations. But the first step in creating a relationship that thrives is recognizing that these myths are just that—myths. They're not universal truths etched in stone; they're malleable ideas that we can, and should, question.

SELF-AWARENESS: THE INVISIBLE GLUE OF LASTING RELATIONSHIPS

"Know thyself." These words, famously inscribed at the Temple of Apollo in Delphi, serve as a timeless reminder of the most important relationship you'll ever have: the one with yourself. It's the relationship that sets the stage for all others, coloring how you interact with your partner, your children, and everyone else in your life.

When you're self-aware, you have a clear perception of your personality, including your strengths, weaknesses, thoughts, beliefs, and emotions. It's like having a mirror for your soul, allowing you to understand how you are seen from the outside world. But let's get real. How many of us can honestly say we've mastered this?

Self-awareness isn't only about knowing who you are but also understanding how your actions and reactions affect those around you—most importantly, your significant other.

Picture that tense dinner table scenario. You know, the one where you're silently seething because your partner forgot to take out the trash again? What's actually making you so angry? Is it the forgotten chore, or is it the perceived lack of respect? And what about your partner's side of the story? Being self-aware can help you dissect these emotional triggers and communicate your feelings more effectively.

You might be wondering, "Am I self-aware?" If you can identify your emotions as they happen, understand the links between your feelings and your actions, and see how your actions affect those around you, then you're on the right path. But don't worry if you're not there yet; this is an ongoing process.

So, how does a lack of self-awareness sabotage relationships? Imagine sailing a ship without understanding the wind direction. You'll probably get somewhere, but chances are it won't be your desired destination. When you're not self-aware, you misinterpret your partner's actions, react impulsively, and then wonder why you're both drowning in emotional chaos. One poor reaction triggers another, setting off a chain reaction that can lead to the downfall of a relationship.

Okay, so you're sold on the idea of becoming more self-aware. Great! But where do you start? Here are ten practical ways to cultivate self-awareness in your relationship:

1. Daily Reflection: Spend a few minutes every day reviewing your interactions and your emotional responses. Were you snappy because you were stressed, or was there another reason?
2. Open Dialogue: Establish a safe space for open, honest communication with your partner. Be willing to both talk and listen.
3. Emotional Vocabulary: Expand your emotional vocabulary. The more precisely you can name your feelings, the better you can manage them.
4. The Pause Button: Before reacting to anything, take a deep breath. This pause can provide invaluable space to assess the situation objectively.
5. Seek Feedback: Don't shy away from asking for your partner's perspective on your actions and behaviors. Sometimes we need an outside perspective to see ourselves more clearly.
6. Nonverbal Cues: Pay attention to body language, both yours and your partner's. Sometimes, what isn't said speaks volumes.
7. Be Your Own Critic: Self-assessment is crucial. Ask yourself challenging questions that require introspection.

8. Identify Patterns: Are there recurring issues or reactions in your relationship? Identifying these can provide insights into what needs to be addressed.
9. Own Your Actions: Acknowledge your mistakes and learn from them. Owning up to your actions is a hallmark of self-awareness.
10. Consult Trusted Advisors: Sometimes you need an outside perspective. Talk to trusted friends or family members about your relationship challenges to gain a new viewpoint.

Wouldn't you like to eliminate that guessing game where you're trying to figure out what your partner "really" means? Or the unnecessary arguments that stem from misunderstandings? By focusing on self-awareness, you can break down those barriers. You'll find that your relationship will feel more like a partnership between two complete individuals rather than two halves trying to make a whole.

RELATIONSHIP ASSESSMENT

You've probably wondered, "Are we compatible?" or "Are we right for each other?" These aren't just questions you ask at the beginning of a relationship; they can pop up at any stage. And they should, because relationships, like people, evolve. So, how can you assess your relationship's strengths and areas that might need a little TLC?

Firstly, you've got to understand that every relationship is a unique blend of two unique individuals. What works for one couple might not work for another. Don't fall for the trap of comparing your relationship to those romantic comedies or even your friends' relationships. You don't need to meet society's cookie-cutter expectations; you need to meet each other's unique needs. That's your golden standard.

Now, onto compatibility. It's not just about sharing hobbies or having great physical chemistry—though those are important. Compatibility is also about aligning on your core values. Do you see eye-to-eye on important issues like finances, family planning, or even your outlook on life? If you're nodding along here, that's a solid foundation to build upon.

Speaking of building, let's discuss pillars. Imagine your relationship as a beautiful structure supported by several pillars. These pillars represent the various facets of your relationship: communication, trust, intimacy, shared goals, and personal space. Examine each pillar carefully. Are they sturdy and strong, or do you see some cracks?

Don't be alarmed by those cracks. We all have them. The key is to identify them before they widen into gaping holes. For instance, if communication is an issue, maybe you need to set aside time to really talk and listen to each other without distractions. If it's intimacy, perhaps a romantic getaway could reignite that spark. Or if it's trust, then it's time to have those hard conversations and rebuild that foundation.

Remember, even within these pillars, uniqueness prevails. Your methods of communication, your expressions of love, and even your little quirks—they all combine to form a relationship that's uniquely yours. So when assessing your relationship, don't use a generic scale. Create your own metrics based on what truly matters to both of you.

WHY WE PICK PEOPLE WHO ARE WRONG FOR US

Probably you've looked back at past relationships and thought, "What was I thinking?" It's a haunting question that digs into the core of our emotions, memories, and self-esteem. We all crave love, acceptance, and companionship, but why do we often find ourselves in relationships with people who are so blatantly wrong for us?

Let's start with the past, a place we often prefer to ignore or gloss over. Our past relationships, family dynamics growing up, and even the friends we kept in our formative years can profoundly impact the choices we make in love. Did your dad have a temper? Chances are, you might be more tolerant of anger in your relationships. Was your mom overly critical? You might find yourself attracted to people who make you feel like you're never good enough. It's a cruel irony, but we often replicate the very environments we should be running from.

Childhood patterns don't just vanish because you're an adult. They stick around, lurking in the background, influencing our decisions in ways we're not even aware of. You might think, "But I'm smarter now, more mature. I can see the red flags." Sure, but the heart has a funny way of overriding logic, especially when it's fueled by deeply ingrained patterns.

So, what types of people are we often drawn to despite knowing better? Let's call these the 'Top 10 Toxic Types'.

First up we have the "Fixer-Upper," someone who you think has so much potential if only they could see it. Newsflash: You can't change people unless they want to change.

Then, there's the "Chronic Cheater," full of apologies and promises to do better—until the next time.

Don't forget the "Emotional Vampire," who sucks the life out of you but keeps you around because you're their emotional crutch.

Or the "Control Freak," who makes you feel like you're walking on eggshells, monitoring your moves and questioning your decisions.

If that's not enough, there's the "Pessimist," the one who always sees the glass half empty and makes you feel like you're carrying the weight of the world.

And how could we forget the "Mama's Boy" or "Daddy's Girl," who never quite cut the umbilical cord and leave you feeling like the third wheel?

Last but not least, the "Manipulator," the one who knows just what to say to make you question your judgment.

Recognize anyone? The truth is, these toxic types are compelling in their twisted ways. They're familiar, and as much as we hate to admit it, familiarity is comforting, even when it's destructive. That's where the trouble begins.

Relationships with toxic individuals often lead to heartbreak, emotional turmoil, and even a cycle of abuse. You might think you can handle it, that it's worth the risk for love. Truth is, it's not always the case.

The key is to break the cycle, acknowledge your patterns, and consciously strive to make better choices. This isn't about blame or judgment; it's about taking control of your love life. You deserve a relationship that uplifts you, challenges you in the best ways, and gives you a sense of peace, not turmoil.

It's high time to turn the page, to move away from the characters that populate your past and toward the ones who will enrich your future. It's not easy, but it's crucial. Your emotional health is at stake, as is your chance for genuine, fulfilling love.

WORKSHEET

Exercises:

1. Identify three common relationship myths you've believed in the past. How have they affected your relationships?

Notes:

_____

_____

_____

2. Reflect on a past or current relationship. How has your level of self-awareness influenced that relationship?

Notes:

_____

_____

_____

3. What insights did you gain from the Relationship Assessment in the chapter?

Notes:

_____

_____

_____

4. Consider why you might be attracted to people who are wrong for you. What patterns can you identify?

Notes:

_____

_____

_____

5. Reflect on how toxic relationships affected your self-esteem and well-being.

Notes:

_____

_____

_____

Practice Questions:

1. What are some common relationship myths, and why are they misleading?

Notes:

_____

_____

_____

2. How does self-awareness contribute to the success of a relationship?

Notes:

_____

_____

_____

3. What is the purpose of a Relationship Assessment, and how can it be useful?

Notes:

_____

_____

_____

4. Why might someone continually choose partners who are wrong for them?

Notes:

_____

_____

_____

5. How can self-awareness help you choose the right partner?

Notes:

_____

_____

_____

Key Takeaways:

1. The importance of debunking relationship myths.

Notes:

_____

_____

_____

2. Self-awareness as a crucial component in relationships.

Notes:

_____

_____

_____

3. The value of Relationship Assessment in understanding your relationship patterns.

Notes:

_____

_____

_____

4. Understanding why we might choose partners who are wrong for us.

Notes:

_____

_____

_____

5. Breaking the cycle of toxic relationships.

Notes:

_____

_____

_____

Action Steps:

1. Identify and challenge any relationship myths you believe in.

Notes:

_____

_____

_____

2. Increase your self-awareness in your relationships.

Notes:

_____

_____

_____

3. Reflect on the Relationship Assessment to understand your relationship patterns.

Notes:

_____

_____

_____

4. Reflect on why you might be choosing the wrong partners and take steps to change this pattern.

Notes:

_____

_____

_____

5. Apply the lessons learned from the chapter to assess and improve your own relationships.

Notes:

_____

_____

_____

Segue

You know, there's something about a sunset that makes you pause and reflect. I remember this one time, standing on the porch, leaning against the wooden railing as the sky transformed into shades of pink and orange. But as magical as that moment was, it was also a stark reminder. Sometimes, we can stand beside someone and feel worlds apart. The sky may be beautiful, but if you can't share what it makes you feel, what's the point?

This realization is the exact reason why we should reflect on our relationships and assess them. Understanding the evolving nature of relationships, the flow of emotions, and the importance of self-discovery within the intricate dance of the connection between partners helps us turn the page and embrace the unknown chapters that lay ahead – a journey where relation-ships would continue to be the heartbeat of our lives.

E - EFFECTIVE RELATIONSHIPS

"The single biggest problem in communication is the illusion that it has taken place."

— GEORGE BERNARD SHAW

Did you know that 65% of divorces are attributed to communication problems? That's more than financial issues, infidelity, or any other commonly cited reason. Let that sink in. It's a startling number, but it underscores just how pivotal effective communication is in maintaining a healthy relationship. It's not just about talking; it's about being understood and understanding your partner in return.

Listening is not merely about being quiet while the other person talks, waiting for your chance to jump in. It's about being present, giving your undivided attention to your partner's words and feelings. It's about asking clarifying questions when you're unsure, and resisting the urge to formulate your response while they're still speaking. Active listening can be exhausting because it requires a lot of emotional and intellectual energy. But the payoff is monumental.

You'd be surprised how often we misinterpret what our partner says. Our personal biases, experiences, and even our mood at the moment can color how we understand their words. Have you ever had an argument where you realize halfway through that you're not even fighting about the same thing? That's a communication breakdown.

But what about those times when emotions run high? The moments when you're so angry or hurt that you can't even think straight, let alone communicate clearly? It's okay to take a break. In fact, taking a step back can be an act of love in itself. It gives both of you the space to breathe, think, and approach the discussion more constructively later on. Just make sure you do come back to resolve the issue; sweeping it under the rug helps no one.

Communicating effectively also involves being honest about your feelings. I'm not just talking about the warm and fuzzy stuff but also the uncomfortable truths. Do you feel unappreciated? Say it. Are you unhappy about your intimacy? Bring it up. The key is to discuss these things without attacking your partner, which is, I know, easier said than done. Frame it in terms of your feelings, and use "I" statements. Instead of saying, "You never spend time with me," try, "I feel lonely when we don't spend quality time together."

Being transparent doesn't mean you must share every single thought that crosses your mind. There's a difference between honesty and oversharing. You don't need to divulge every little detail of your day or share thoughts that might be unnecessarily hurtful. Transparency is about being open with the things that matter, the things that affect both of you and the relationship.

An often underestimated facet of interpersonal interaction is the art of nonverbal communication. The messages delivered through one's body language, tone of voice, and facial expressions can frequently convey more meaning than spoken words. It can be remarkably instructive to itemize such nonverbal cues. Here is a contemplative look at some of these cues:

- Eye Rolling: A dismissive gesture that can signal disdain or frustration, often conveying messages unintended by the speaker.
- Dismissive Tone: This tone can unintentionally send signals of indifference or contempt, hindering effective communication.
- Tense Posture: An indication of stress or discomfort that can reflect underlying emotions or thoughts that are not being verbally expressed.
- Facial Expressions: A smirk, a frown, a raised eyebrow— all of these can communicate emotions and thoughts without a single word being uttered.
- Touch: A simple touch can often breach the barriers that words cannot, expressing comfort, understanding, or empathy.
- Shared Look: Exchanging glances can be a form of silent conversation, expressing mutual understanding or shared feelings without verbal articulation.

By recognizing these cues, we can be more attuned to the unspoken messages we are emitting and receiving, cultivating a richer, more empathic level of interaction. It is essential to cultivate an awareness of such nonverbal cues, both exhibited and perceived, as comprehension is often achieved not just through verbal exchange, but also through these subtle, yet profound, forms of communication.

IF YOU DON'T USE YOUR WORDS, YOU WILL FAIL AT RELATIONSHIPS

Why do we often assume that our partners, the people who supposedly know us best, can magically interpret our innermost thoughts and feelings? It's a trap many of us fall into, believing that love equates to some sort of psychic connection. You've seen it in movies, read it in novels—the notion that true love somehow endows us with the extraordinary ability to understand each other without uttering a word. It's romantic, but let's get real—it's also a recipe for disaster.

This unspoken expectation sets the stage for disappointment, resentment, and, ultimately, failed relationships. Silence, while golden in some contexts, can be toxic in a relationship that requires open dialogue to thrive. Love is not a game of charades; it's a partnership that demands explicit communication.

It's tempting to think that your partner should just "get you" without you having to spell everything out. But let's flip the script for a moment. How fair is it to place such an onus on them? Even the most intuitive among us can't fully grasp the complexities of another person's emotional landscape. The assumption that "if they love me, they'll just know," not only sets your partner up for failure but also sets you up for perpetual disappointment.

Recognizing that neither you nor your partner can read minds is paramount. The challenge then arises—how does one convey thoughts and emotions in a manner that is both productive and clear? The initial step is to abandon indistinct language and obscure suggestions. Articulate your emotions and the reasoning behind them with clarity and precision. Providing more illustrative examples can be illuminative:

Instead of: "You never listen to me,"

Try Saying: "I feel unheard when I share my thoughts, and it seems like my opinions are overlooked."

Instead of: "You're always late,"

Try Saying: "When you arrive late, it gives me the impression that my time isn't valued."

Instead of: "You should know why I'm upset,"

Try Saying: "I felt hurt when you canceled our plans, making me feel unimportant."

Instead of: "You don't care about my feelings,"

Try Saying: "Your actions make me feel neglected and make me question your concern for my emotions."

Each of these revised statements not only communicates the speaker's feelings more clearly but also places the emphasis on those feelings rather than assigning blame. This approach encourages a more open and constructive dialogue, where both partners feel heard and understood, fostering a healthier and more harmonious relationship.

The importance of timing cannot be overstated. It's imperative to address underlying issues, but articulating them impulsively in the midst of heightened emotions can often lead to less-than-optimal outcomes. It is during these heated moments that our ability to communicate efficiently is usually compromised, and we find ourselves uttering words steeped in frustration and anger, words that we would not consider voicing in a more composed state of mind.

When emotions run high, our communicative intentions can become clouded by the turmoil of the moment, releasing a torrent of unnecessary and often hurtful statements. We tend to lose sight of resolution and become conduits for the unchecked expression of our discontent. It's crucial to recognize such situations and to make a conscious effort to step back, to allow the turbulent emotions to subside, and to approach the conversation with a clear, calm mind.

By doing so, we enable more constructive dialogues where the focus is on understanding and resolution rather than on the release of pent-up emotions. In these calmer, more reflective states, we can communicate our thoughts and feelings more effectively, fostering a deeper understanding and a more harmonious interaction.

Choose a time when both of you can have an undistracted conversation. Open up, but also be prepared to listen. Communication is a two-way street, and understanding each other requires both speaking and listening with genuine intent.

ACTIVE LISTENING

When you're genuinely tuned in to what your partner is saying, you're not just hearing words; you're feeling the emotions behind those words. Think of it as a two-for-one deal: you get the message and a deeper understanding of what your partner is going through. Now, who wouldn't want that?

Active listening isn't just about the speaker; it's equally about the listener. It's about giving your full attention, asking clarifying questions, and offering verbal and nonverbal cues to show you're engaged. It's the kind of listening that makes the speaker feel seen, heard, and, most importantly, understood.

Why is this so crucial in relationships, you ask? Well, when conflicts arise, active listening becomes your secret weapon. Imagine you're in the middle of a heated argument. Tempers are flaring, and words are flying like arrows. Instead of dodging and shooting back, what if you paused and really listened? That simple act can defuse tension like nothing else. You're taking the first step towards resolution by showing your willingness to understand.

But the benefits don't stop at conflict resolution. Active listening builds trust. Consistent showing that you're fully present during conversations creates a safe space for openness and vulnerability.

Over time, this strengthens the trust between you and your partner, creating a virtuous cycle of communication.

Ah, but there's a catch. Active listening is not something you master overnight. It's a skill, and like any skill, it requires practice. Yes, you'll mess up, you'll zone out, and you might even interrupt a few times. That's okay. What matters is your intention to improve and the effort you put into it.

Here's a quick tip for those moments when you find your mind wandering. Picture a stop sign. This mental imagery can jolt you back into the moment. Another trick is to paraphrase what your partner is saying. It confirms that you're paying attention and gives them a chance to clarify if you've misunderstood something.

Now, the balance of active listening should go both ways. It's as much your right to be heard as it is your responsibility to listen. If you find that you're the one always lending an ear but not getting the same in return, it's time for an open conversation with your partner.

The aim here isn't to keep score but to foster a balanced relationship where both of you feel equally valued and understood. It's about co-creating a space where you can lay down your burdens, knowing they'll be picked up with care and respect.

TOP THINGS EVERY COUPLE SHOULD DISCUSS

You've probably sat across from your partner at some point, and wondered, "Do we really know each other as deeply as we think?" Sure, you know their coffee order, their favorite movie, and how they take their eggs. But do you know their fears? Their dreams? The intricate layers of their values and expectations?

Values

Ah, values—the bedrock of any meaningful relationship. They're like the invisible thread stitching your lives together. You may both value family, but how does that look in action? For one, family might mean gathering for Sunday dinners, while for the other, it's about unfiltered conversations over late-night snacks. See, the devil's in the details, and that's where you both need to vibe. Keep revisiting this conversation; people change, and so do their values.

Boundaries

Boundaries are the unsung heroes of a relationship. They're not walls; think of them more like guidelines. Discuss your emotional and physical boundaries. It could be anything from your comfort level with social media sharing to how you'd like to spend holidays. Respect for each other's boundaries is an unspoken love language.

Likes and Dislikes

Ah, the spice of life! Knowing each other's likes and dislikes adds a flair of thoughtfulness to the relationship. You don't have to be a clone of your partner, but recognizing what makes them tick (or ticked off) can help you avoid unnecessary bumps on the road. Also, discovering new likes and dislikes together can be a thrilling adventure.

Needs and Wants

What you need and what you want from your partner might not always align, and that's perfectly okay. The key is in the negotiation. For instance, I need quality time with my partner; it's non-negotiable. On the other hand, I want an annual vacation, but it's not a deal-breaker. It's essential to separate these for a clearer picture of how you both can fulfill each other's needs and wants.

What Makes Them Happy

Happiness is the heartbeat of a relationship. It's not just about grand gestures or expensive gifts. Sometimes, it's the little things, like making coffee for them in the morning or listening with enthusiasm, when they speak. These small acts are the building blocks of happiness in a relationship.

Let's not forget the fun factor! A relationship isn't an endless loop of deep talks and problem-solving. Plan for fun—be it a spontaneous weekend getaway, a cooking challenge, or binge-watching a new series. These moments of levity infuse fresh energy into your relationship.

NONVERBAL COMMUNICATION

You've probably heard the old saying that actions speak louder than words. In a relationship, this couldn't be more accurate. Communication isn't just about talking; it's also about listening. And listening isn't just about hearing the words; it's about absorbing the full spectrum of human expression. Our bodies often say what words cannot. The way you stand, the way you look at someone, even the tone of your voice—all these things contribute to the message you're sending.

Ever had one of those heated discussions where, no matter what you said, it seemed like your partner wasn't getting it? Yeah, we've all been there. You can articulate your thoughts flawlessly, but if your body language is screaming something else, you're essentially tossing those words into a blazing fire.

Let's break it down, shall we? Imagine you're apologizing for forgetting your anniversary. You say you're sorry, but your arms are crossed, and you avoid eye contact. Even if you claim to be apologetic, your body language tells a different story. Your partner might see your actions as a sign of insincerity or indifference. Not the ideal way to mend fences.

Think about those times when you've had to discuss sensitive topics. Maybe it's finances or maybe it's a decision about relocating for work. No matter how carefully you choose your words, your body language and tone can make or break the conversation.

Nonverbal cues can be particularly telling in emotionally charged situations. Consider the simple act of holding hands. When your partner's grip tightens, it's often an unspoken reassurance that they're there for you. Or how about when you caught your loved one staring at you from across the room, and that look alone made you feel like the most cherished person on Earth?

Then there's tone. Ah, the way you say something can often be as impactful as what you're saying. Even the most affectionate "I love you" can lose its charm if said in a sarcastic or dismissive tone. Conversely, a well-timed sigh or a soft touch can turn a mundane interaction into a moment to remember.

Now, you're probably thinking, "Great, another thing to worry about when I'm already navigating the complex labyrinth of love." But fear not! Being aware of your nonverbal cues doesn't mean you have to become a mime artist or a body language expert. It just means that you need to be more conscious of how your actions—or lack thereof—might be interpreted.

How about we start with the basics? *Eye contact*. It's an age-old technique but incredibly effective. Looking directly into your partner's eyes when speaking shows engagement and sincerity. It says, "I'm here, I'm present, and what you're saying matters to me." But be mindful, there's a fine line between intense eye contact and an uncomfortable stare—don't cross it.

Touch is another powerful nonverbal communicator. A warm hug, a gentle pat on the back, or a tender kiss can say more than a thousand words. It's not just about the physical touch but the emotion and intention behind it. That's what makes the difference.

Gestures, too, can add layers of meaning to your interactions. Remember how your heart skipped a beat the first time your partner brushed their fingers through your hair? It wasn't just a casual touch; it was a gesture loaded with affection, and it made you feel special.

Of course, I'd be remiss not to mention the power of *facial expressions*. A smile, a frown, a raised eyebrow—they all convey emotions more vividly than any words can. Have you ever noticed how a genuine smile from your loved one can instantly lift your spirits? That's the power of nonverbal communication at work.

And let's not forget *posture*. The way you carry yourself speaks volumes about your confidence and how you feel in a given situation. Standing tall with your shoulders back not only makes you appear more confident but also shows that you're engaged in the relationship. Slouching or looking down, on the other hand, can convey disinterest or insecurity.

But let's flip the coin and talk about positive nonverbal cues, the ones that make your heart soar. A spontaneous hug from behind while you're cooking, a wink across a crowded room, or the way your partner's eyes light up when you walk through the door. These gestures may be small, but their impact on a relationship is immeasurable. They are the threads that weave the fabric of a deeply connected, mutually satisfying relationship. They serve as affirmations of love and respect, building a reservoir of goodwill that can help see you through tougher times.

Imagine the power of applying this understanding daily. You'd become more adept at navigating the complexities of emotional landscapes, not just in romantic relationships but also in friendships and even work relationships. It's like having a decoder ring for human emotions.

But hold on, before you start making assumptions about nonverbal cues, remember that context is crucial. A smile doesn't always signify happiness; sometimes, it's a mask for discomfort or insecurity. A hug isn't always an expression of warmth; it could be a way to assert control. So, understanding the context is crucial in interpreting nonverbal communication effectively.

It takes time and effort to attune yourself to the nuances of body language, facial expressions, and tone. It's an ongoing process, a skill that you'll continue to refine throughout your life. So don't beat yourself up if you don't get it right immediately. The key is to remain aware and make a conscious effort to understand these unspoken signals.

Effective communication is the cornerstone of any healthy relationship. While spoken words are undeniably important, nonverbal cues offer another layer of complexity that can enrich interactions with your significant other. They can serve as a catalyst for deeper connection, greater understanding, and ultimately, a more fulfilling relationship. If you can master the art of nonverbal communication, you're well on your way to a relationship that's not just good, but extraordinary.

WORKSHEET

Exercises:

1. Reflect on a recent conversation you had. Did you actively listen? Write down what you noticed about your listening habits.

Notes:

_____

_____

_____

2. List down the top things you believe every couple should discuss. Compare it with the book's suggestions.

Notes:

_____

_____

_____

3. Think of a situation where nonverbal communication played a significant role. Describe the situation and the nonverbal cues.

Notes:

_____

_____

_____

4. Recall a relationship that failed because of poor communication. What could have been done differently?

Notes:

_____

_____

_____

5. Identify the key factors that contribute to effective communication.

Notes:

_____

_____

_____

Practice Questions:

1. Why is active listening essential in maintaining effective relationships?

Notes:

_____

_____

_____

2. What are some nonverbal communication cues that can affect a conversation?

Notes:

_____

_____

_____

3. How can poor communication lead to the failure of relationships?

Notes:

_____

_____

_____

4. What are the top things every couple should discuss, according to the book?

Notes:

_____

_____

_____

5. Why is it important to approach any conversation with a clear, calm mind?

Notes:

_____

_____

_____

Key Takeaways:

1. The importance of active listening in maintaining effective relationships.

Notes:

_____

_____

_____

2. Nonverbal communication cues can significantly impact conversations and relationships.

Notes:

_____

_____

_____

3. Poor communication can lead to the failure of relationships.

Notes:

_____

_____

_____

4. There are key topics that every couple should discuss to maintain a healthy relationship.

Notes:

_____

_____

_____

5. Listening with your eyes and heart is as important as listening with your ears.

Notes:

_____

_____

_____

Action Steps:

1. Practice active listening in your next conversation.

Notes:

_____

_____

_____

2. Pay attention to nonverbal cues in your next interaction.

Notes:

_____

_____

_____

3. Identify areas of communication that need improvement in your relationships and create a plan to address them.

Notes:

_____

_____

_____

4. Discuss the top things mentioned in the book with your partner.

Notes:

_____

_____

_____

5. Find the nonverbal cues and discuss them with your partner.

Notes:

_____

_____

_____

Segue

As we've delved into the realm of effective relationships, it's essential to recognize that the intricacies of human connection are both fascinating and complex. In this chapter, we have explored the multifaceted dimensions of effective relationships, from fostering open communication and cultivating active listening, to discussing the topics that are fundamental for any effective relationships.

Now let's venture into the heart of any relationship, the realm of love and intimacy. Love, that force that binds us together, and intimacy, the sacred space where souls intertwine and vulnerabilities are shared. In this chapter, we'll navigate the labyrinth of emotions. From the electric spark of a new romance to the enduring flame of lifelong partnerships, we'll uncover the ingredients that foster deep connection and passion. So, let us embark on this voyage of the heart.

L - LOVE AND INTIMACY

"Love is not about possession; love is about appreciation."

— OSHO

Love and intimacy are the lifeblood of any relationship, but it's easy to forget that amidst the daily grind of life. We get so caught up in chores, kids, work that we forget to nourish the one relationship that should be our sanctuary from all that stress. We stop holding hands. We stop kissing. We stop talking—really talking—about how our day went or what we're feeling.

So, what builds love and intimacy, and what breaks it down?

WHAT BUILDS UP LOVE

Building love is not just about grand gestures or romantic getaways—though those are nice. It's about the little things. A simple "I love you" text in the middle of a busy day, remembering to buy their favorite snack when you're grocery shopping, or even just washing the dishes when it's not your turn. These acts might seem trivial, but they're the building blocks of a lasting relationship.

Being emotionally available is crucial. How often do you sit down and talk with your partner about your hopes and fears? Do you listen when they need to vent or offer a shoulder to cry on? Emotional intimacy is the backbone of a strong relationship.

Respecting each other's personal space is another factor. It's important to have your own interests, your own friends, and your own time. This not only enriches your individual lives but also brings new energy into your relationship.

What Breaks Down Love

Now let's talk about what can erode love. *Jealousy*, for one, is a major culprit. The moment you start questioning your partner's actions or intentions, you're cracking the foundation of your relationship. Jealousy stems from insecurity, and insecurity can kill love like nothing else.

Another thing that can seriously undermine love is **neglect**. It could be neglecting your partner's emotional needs or even just neglecting to say thank you for the little things they do. Neglect is the silent killer of relationships because it's so easy to overlook. You think everything is fine until one day, it's not.

And then there's the issue of **dishonesty**. A single lie can break trust, and rebuilding that trust is a Herculean task. Transparency is key, my friends. In a relationship, dishonesty is not a sin of commission but a sin of omission. When you hide something from your partner, you're essentially saying they're unworthy of your truth.

The Importance of Intimacy

So why is intimacy—emotional, physical, or otherwise—so important in a relationship? Simple. *Intimacy creates a safe space where both partners can be their true selves without fear of judgment.* It's where you can share your deepest secrets, wildest fantasies, and most painful traumas, and still feel loved and accepted. Intimacy is like a cozy blanket on a cold winter night. It gives you warmth, comfort, and a sense of belonging.

Physical intimacy is equally important. And I'm not just talking about sex, though that's a part of it. I mean the little things—like cuddling on the couch, holding hands while watching a movie, or hugging each other after a long day. These acts of physical intimacy are not just about pleasure; they're also about communicating love and building a deeper emotional connection.

So, the next time you find yourself caught up in the day-to-day routine, take a step back. Look at your partner and remember the reasons you fell in love in the first place. Ask yourself: when was the last time you did something to nurture that love?

Remember, a relationship is like a garden. If you don't water the plants, they'll wither and die. So, make sure you're watering your relationship with love and intimacy. It's worth it.

EMOTIONAL INTIMACY

When we talk about emotional intimacy, it's tempting to think it's some magical thing that happens when two people are deeply in love. But the truth is, emotional intimacy is a cultivated garden, not a wild forest. It takes work, consistent nurturing, and, yes, a dollop of courage.

Vulnerability: The Gateway to Emotional Intimacy

Vulnerability is the cornerstone of emotional intimacy. It's about letting your guard down and showing the real you. But here's the catch: Being vulnerable isn't about spilling your guts on the first date or oversharing. It's about intentional, measured openness. Think of it as opening the windows of your soul but with screens still in place. You let the fresh air in, but you also have boundaries.

It's okay to start small. You don't have to reveal your darkest secrets immediately. Try sharing something personal but less risky. Notice how your partner responds. Do they listen empathetically? Do they open up in return? This reciprocal dance gradually builds a strong emotional connection that can withstand the test of time.

Empathy: The Glue that Holds Relationships Together

Empathy is often underestimated, but it's the adhesive that binds emotional intimacy. When your partner shares something vulnerable, listen. Hold off on judgments or solutions. The goal is not to fix but to understand. Empathy transcends words; it's a heartfelt connection that says, "I'm here, and I get you."

Sometimes empathy means sitting together in silence, offering a comforting touch, or simply acknowledging the other person's feelings. It's a skill one can develop and hone over time. And the more you practice it, the more you'll find that empathy not only deepens your emotional intimacy but also equips you to navigate the choppy waters of conflict and misunderstanding.

Shared Experiences: The Threads that Weave a Strong Emotional Fabric

Creating shared experiences is like adding patches to a quilt. Each experience, whether big or small, adds a new layer of depth and richness to your relationship. It could be as simple as cooking dinner together on a Friday night or as grand as back-packing through Europe. The scale doesn't matter; the emotional imprint does.

But be cautious. Not all shared experiences contribute positively to emotional intimacy. Some experiences, like going through hardship or facing adversity together, can either deepen your connection or drive a wedge between you. The key lies in how you both handle these situations. Do you turn towards each other for support, or do you isolate and turn away? The former can be a powerful catalyst for emotional closeness, while the latter can erode it quickly.

Quality of Communication

Having a marathon heart-to-heart conversation once a year isn't going to cut it. Emotional intimacy thrives on regular, quality interactions. It's the small, daily moments of connection that accumulate into a strong emotional bond. Take time each day to check in with each other. It doesn't have to be an hour-long conversation; even a few minutes can make a difference. Ask about each other's day, share something that made you smile, or discuss future plans. Keep the emotional lines of communication open and flowing.

Establishing a Safe Emotional Space

Creating a safe emotional space is crucial for nurturing intimacy. This is a zone where both you and your partner can be your authentic selves without fear of judgment or criticism. It's a sanctuary where your innermost thoughts and feelings are not only accepted but also valued. And in this sacred space, emotional intimacy flourishes.

PHYSICAL INTIMACY: TECHNIQUES AND TABOOS

Do you ever notice how every touch is electric at the start of a relationship? Every hug a promise, every kiss an escape? But as time marches on, even the most passionate couples find that the electricity can dim. It's not a sign of diminished love, no. It's just life getting in the way. Yet, let's get real: the physical aspect of your relationship is a crucial facet of your overall emotional well-being for both of you.

When it comes to physical intimacy, there are two roads: the things that ignite the spark and the things that douse it. It's essential to understand both because, let's face it, the last thing you want is to turn your partner off when you're trying to keep the home fires burning.

The Turn-Offs: Men vs. Women

To keep things neat and easy to follow, think of this as a table of sorts, albeit without the rows and columns.

Men's Turn-Offs:

- Emotional Unavailability: A lack of emotional connection can lead to a lack of physical connection.
- Nagging: No one finds constant criticism attractive.
- Rudeness: Nobody likes rude people, period.
- Selfishness: Selfishness refers to a lack of consideration for the needs and feelings of others.
- Parenting behavior: A man typically wants to be treated as an equal partner, and having an idea of a second mother as a partner does not translate into a physical attraction.
- Poor Personal Hygiene: This one should be self-explanatory.

- Negative mindset: Men find a positive mindset more attractive because they subconsciously know their partner's positivity will also affect their well-being.

Women's Turn-Offs:

- Lack of Foreplay: Romance often starts long before the bedroom.
- Selfishness: A partner only concerned with their own pleasure isn't a turn-on.
- Being Ignored: Feeling emotionally sidelined is a big no-no.
- Lack of compliments: Compliments significantly boost self-esteem, confidence, and overall well-being, especially in women.
- Rudeness: Just as rude women for men, rude men for women is always a no.
- Poor hygiene: Women are especially sensitive to odors and appearances. An adult male unable to take care of the basics of hygiene will likely not ignite a spark.
- Jealousy: It can be a huge turn-off for women as an indication of a lack of trust.

While these are broad generalizations, they're backed by multiple sources, including articles from TheList.com, Everyday Health, and YourTango. As well as about physicality, it's also about the emotional and mental buildup.

Having navigated through the aspects of what should be avoided, let's pivot our attention to reviving the connection and intimacy. You might be familiar with Gary Chapman's Five Love Languages which include:

Words of Affirmation
Quality Time
Receiving Gifts
Acts of Service
Physical Touch

These languages offer insight into how we express and receive love. However, for the context of our discussion, we will delve deeper and concentrate on one of these languages, the 'Physical Touch', giving it a more comprehensive exploration to understand its nuances and significance in fostering closeness and connection.

Sensual Skills 101

First, *communication*. Yes, it's cliche, but how do you know what your partner enjoys if you don't talk about it? And I'm not just talking about a shy whisper in the dark. Have an open, honest, and—yes—awkward conversation about your desires and fears. It opens doors we didn't know were closed.

Second, *variety* is the spice of life. Remember that old saying? It's old for a reason. Changing up your routine can infuse your relationship with a new sense of excitement and anticipation. It could be as simple as kissing differently or as adventurous as introducing new sensations and experiences into your intimate moments.

Third, *spontaneity*. I can't stress enough how important a surprise hug, kiss, or any form of touch can be. It's like a sudden shower in a drought. Spontaneity can resurrect feelings that you thought were long buried.

Fourth, **playfulness.** Try incorporating humor and light-heartedness into your interactions. You may be surprised how much joy playfulness can bring into your shared experiences.

Firth, **respect.** When you respect your partner's desires and most intimate dreams and they do so in return, then you truly create a sacred space for each other to enjoy your moments of intimacy.

Sixth, **patience.** It may be hard to fully open up to someone, even your loved one, however with a little patience, you can build a strong and fulfilling intimate connection with your partner over time.

Sensual skills are not about following a strict set of rules but rather about being attuned to your partner's needs and fostering a deeper connection. Communication is key, and being open and receptive to feedback is crucial for growth in this area. Every individual and relationship is unique, so it's essential to tailor these skills to suit the specific dynamics of your partnership.

WORKSHEET

Exercises:

1. What are the key components of emotional intimacy, according to the chapter? How can you apply these in your relationship?

Notes:

_____

_____

_____

2. How does physical intimacy strengthen a relationship, as per the chapter? What are some techniques mentioned?

Notes:

_____

_____

_____

3. Thinking of the question: "Are you cohabiting with a stranger or living with a life partner?" What does this mean to you, and how does it apply to your current situation?

Notes:

_____

_____

4. Discuss the taboos related to physical intimacy. How can understanding these taboos help improve your relationship?

Notes:

_____

_____

_____

5. How can you build up love in a relationship, according to the chapter? What steps can you take?

Notes:

_____

_____

_____

Practice questions:

1. What is emotional intimacy, and how does it differ from physical intimacy?

Notes:

_____

_____

_____

2. What are a few techniques to build physical intimacy?

Notes:

_____

_____

_____

3. What does cohabiting with a stranger mean in the context of a relationship?

Notes:

_____

_____

_____

4. What are some taboos of physical intimacy mentioned in the chapter?

Notes:

_____

_____

_____

5. What are some strategies suggested to build up love in a relationship?

Notes:

_____

_____

_____

Key Takeaways:

1. Little everyday acts of love might seem trivial, but they're the building blocks of a lasting relationship.

Notes:

_____

_____

_____

2. Physical and emotional intimacy are equally important.

Notes:

_____

_____

_____

3. Mastering your sensual skills is crucial to foster a deeper connection.

Notes:

_____

_____

_____

4. Quality of communication affects the levels of your emotional intimacy.

Notes:

_____

_____

_____

5. When it comes to physical intimacy, there are the things that ignite the spark and the things that douse it.

Notes:

_____

_____

_____

Action Steps:

1. Discuss the fundamentals of love building with your partner.

Notes:

_____

_____

_____

2. Think of the ways you cultivate the garden of your emotional intimacy.

Notes:

_____

_____

_____

3. Discuss the top things mentioned in the chapter with your partner.

Notes:

_____

_____

_____

4. Have an open conversation about your physical intimacy aspects.

Notes:

_____

_____

_____

5. Have an open conversation about what turns you on and off.

Notes:

_____

_____

_____

Segue

We're all human, and, let's face it, none of us are relationship experts when we start. Even after years of being together, we all have our moments. It's not about the absence of problems but how we address them when they inevitably arise.

Speaking of hearts, let's not forget the role of emotional and physical intimacy. Over time, the spark that initially drew you together might seem to dim, but that doesn't mean it's gone. It just needs a little kindling. Small gestures like surprise hugs, random "I love you" messages or even a simple touch can reignite the emotional connection you share. And please, don't underestimate the power of a passionate kiss; it's not just for teenagers.

Physical intimacy is the language that transcends words, a channel of communication that brings you closer in the most primal way. But let's be real; maintaining that level of physical connection is hard, especially with work, kids, and the hustle and bustle of daily life. The key is to prioritize it. Put it on your calendar if you have to! Make time for intimacy just as you would for any other important aspect of your life.

In our pursuit of love and connection, let's not forget about the individual identities that make us who we are. Personal growth should not be a solo journey but one that you take together, hand in hand, as you both evolve and adapt. Remember, a relationship consists of two complete individuals, not two halves trying to make a whole.

A - ADDRESSING THE ISSUES

"A man's character may be learned from the adjectives which he habitually uses in conversation."

— MARK TWAIN

You know that scene in movies where couples are shouting at each other, throwing accusations like they're in a courtroom drama, and then suddenly, one of them has an epiphany? In real life the epiphany part takes a lot more patience and persistence than Hollywood usually shows.

So, why do minor disagreements often lead to significant conflicts? Because they're not just about the issue at hand; they're a symptom of deeper problems, the proverbial tip of the iceberg.

Issues in a relationship are like weeds in a garden. Ignore them, and they grow, stealing nutrients from the beautiful flowers you've worked so hard to cultivate. These 'weeds' can manifest in various ways: communication breakdowns, lack of intimacy, and even the perpetual battle over household chores. The more we ignore these issues, the more they fester and grow, eventually causing irreversible damage to the relationship.

Want to liberate yourself from the circle of recurring, unsettled disputes? Let's dissect this process into several structured steps for better clarity and application:

Identify the Core Issue

Begin by pinpointing the root of the contention. Is the actual concern the dishwasher, or does it stem from a more profound need for control, acknowledgment, or comprehension? Recognizing the fundamental problem is a stepping stone to addressing it effectively.

Select an Appropriate Time and Setting

Find the right moment and place to start the conversation. Seek a neutral territory where both parties can express freely, devoid of disruptions or interpositions.

Practice Active Listening

This is a pivotal component. During disputes, our primary focus tends to be on voicing our perspectives, overshadowing the need to heed what our counterpart is articulating. Active listening necessitates absolute concentration, comprehension, response, and recollection of the counterpart's discourse. It involves offering unreserved attention, inquiring for elucidation, and giving feedback.

Ensure Follow-Through

Post-compromise, it's imperative to enact any concurred-upon alterations or actions. Uniformity is the best approach to demonstrate your devotion to resolving conflicts and enhancing the relationship's quality.

By adhering to these well-organized steps, we can break the cycle of repetitive arguments and cultivate a more harmonious and understanding relationship dynamic.

But what if the issue is something that can't be compromised on? In such cases, it's essential to evaluate the overall health and future of the relationship. Is this a deal-breaker, or can it be overlooked for the sake of all the good in the relationship? This is a deeply personal decision that may require considerable thought and possibly even outside counsel.

CONFLICT RESOLUTION: THE ART OF MAKING PEACE

In the heat of an argument, the room turns into a furnace, and words become arrows. The adrenaline surges, and before you know it, things are said that can't be taken back. But rest assured, that is not the end of the world. That conflict doesn't have to be a boxing ring but can be a dance floor where you and your partner find rhythm in your discord.

You know that sensation when you're so deeply engrossed in what someone is saying that the world around you blurs? That's active listening. But let's be honest, it's easier said than done. It's one thing to nod and throw in the occasional "uh-huh," but it's another to genuinely absorb what your partner is saying— emotionally and intellectually. You're not just catching words; you're capturing feelings, meanings, and the nuances that dance between the lines.

You see, we're often too fixated on our viewpoint, guarding it like a treasure. But a relationship is less like a battleground and more like a shared garden. The essence of finding common ground is in unearthing that shared soil, where both can plant seeds of agreement. It's not just about approving to make peace but about understanding each other's perspectives so profoundly that you find a shared vision. And sometimes, that means stepping into your partner's shoes and walking around in them.

Now, let's talk about compromise, that magical realm where both parties bend a little, but neither breaks. The word itself has been stigmatized as 'settling for less,' but let's debunk that myth. Compromise is not about diluting your essence; it's about concocting a new brew that has a flavor of both. It's like cooking a meal together; maybe you like it spicy, and they prefer it mild. You find a recipe that meets both your palettes. Compromise is that secret ingredient that makes both of you say, "Wow, this is delicious."

It can't be stressed enough how conflict resolution is less about winning and more about understanding. It's not about scoring points; it's about scoring a deeper connection, a stronger bond, and a happier life together.

You see, every relationship has its share of friction. But it's how you handle that friction that determines whether it'll cause a fire or warm your hearts. With the right approach, even the toughest conflicts can lead to richer, more robust relationships.

We have addressed active listening, open communication, and compromises as pillars of conflict resolution, but let's dive deeper and list some effective conflict resolution techniques:

1. Empathy:

- Try to understand the emotions and concerns of the other person. Empathy can create a connection and make it easier to find common ground.

2. Stay Calm:

- Keep your emotions in check during the discussion. Take deep breaths if needed, and avoid reacting impulsively. A calm demeanor can contribute to a more constructive conversation.

3. Clarify Misunderstandings:

- Ensure that both parties have a clear understanding of the issues involved. Misunderstandings can often be a source of conflict, and clarifying them can prevent further disputes.

4. Focus on the Issue, Not the Person:

- Separate the problem from the person. Avoid personal attacks and instead concentrate on the specific issue causing the conflict.

5. Find Common Ground:

- Identify areas where you both agree and build on those points. This helps create a positive atmosphere and a foundation for resolving the conflict.

6. Brainstorm Solutions:

- Work together to generate potential solutions. Be open-minded and creative in exploring different options that could satisfy both parties.

7. Use "I" Statements:

- Frame your concerns using "I" statements to avoid sounding accusatory. Instead of saying, "You never listen to me," try, "I feel unheard when you interrupt me." It's a subtle shift but one that puts you both on the same team, fighting the problem rather than each other.

8. Take a Break if Necessary:

- If emotions are running high and the conversation becomes unproductive, it's okay to take a break. Allow some time for both parties to cool down before returning to the discussion.

Remember that conflicts are a natural part of relationships, and the goal is not always to eliminate them but to manage and resolve them in a healthy way.

FORGIVENESS AND HEALING

Forgiveness isn't just a word you utter before you move on. It's a conscious, deliberate decision to release feelings of resentment or vengeance toward someone who has harmed you. It doesn't mean forgetting or condoning the wrongdoing, but it does mean letting go of the emotional burden you carry.

Remember the last time you forgave someone? How it felt like taking off a heavy backpack you didn't even know you were carrying? Forgiveness frees you, but it also has a ripple effect on your relationships, particularly the one with your significant other.

For many of us, past conflicts are like old, forgotten coffee stains on a once pristine rug. They might fade with time, but they're never really gone. And let's face it: in a relationship, these stains can accumulate quickly, turning your vibrant tapestry of love into a mottled mess. Here's where forgiveness comes into play. It's the powerful detergent that removes those stains and restores the rug's original brilliance.

But let's not get it twisted; forgiveness isn't a one-off act. It's more like a muscle that needs constant exercise. The more you forgive, the easier it becomes to let go of trivial issues and focus on building a healthier relationship. Think of it as relationship cardio, keeping your emotional heart in good shape.

You may wonder why forgiveness is so essential in sustaining a relationship. Well, holding onto grudges creates emotional distance. It's like building a wall, brick by brick, with each unresolved issue and unspoken resentment. Before you know it, this wall becomes an insurmountable barrier that disconnects you from your loved one.

When you choose to forgive, you pave the way for healing. Healing isn't just about patching up old wounds; it's about creating a stronger, more resilient bond. When you've been through the thick and thin of emotional turmoil and come out stronger, that's when you realize the incredible resilience of your relationship.

And you know what's amazing? This cycle of forgiveness and healing fosters emotional safety. When you feel safe emotionally, you're more likely to be honest, transparent, and vulnerable. And isn't that what we all crave in a relationship? An emotional sanctuary where we can be our true selves without fear of judgment or rejection.

But hold on, what about serious breaches of trust, like infidelity or deceit? Well, forgiveness in these situations is a complex, often lengthy process. It may require professional guidance and a significant period for introspection. Sometimes, you may forgive but decide that continuing the relationship is not in your best interest, and that's perfectly okay. The essential part is that you've freed yourself from the emotional shackles that were holding you back.

Forgiving others can be a challenging but important process for personal growth and well-being. Here are some strategies that may help:

1. Understand the Benefits of Forgiveness:

- Recognize that forgiveness is for your own benefit, not necessarily for the person who wronged you. It can free you from the burden of anger and resentment.

2. Empathy:

- Try to understand the perspective of the person who hurt you. Consider their motivations, circumstances, and the possibility that they may not have intended to cause harm.

3. Release Negative Emotions:

- Express your emotions in a healthy way, whether through talking to a friend, journaling, or engaging in activities that help release negative energy.

4. Acceptance:

- Accept that people make mistakes. No one is perfect, and everyone has flaws. Acknowledge the imperfections in yourself and others.

5. Time and Healing:

- Forgiveness is a process that takes time. Allow yourself the necessary time to heal and process your emotions before attempting to forgive.

6. Set Boundaries:

- Establish clear boundaries to protect yourself from future harm. This doesn't mean cutting off all contact, but it's important to create a healthy distance if needed.

7. Seek Support:

- Talk to friends, family, or a therapist about your feelings. Sharing your thoughts and emotions can provide valuable perspectives and support.

8. Focus on the Present:

- Concentrate on the present moment and the positive aspects of your life. Dwelling on the past can hinder your ability to forgive and move forward.

9. Self-Reflection:

- Reflect on your own mistakes and times when you've been forgiven. Understanding the reciprocal nature of forgiveness can make it easier to extend to others.

10. Choose Forgiveness:

- Ultimately, forgiveness is a choice. Make a conscious decision to let go of the resentment and anger. This doesn't mean condoning the actions but rather releasing the emotional hold they have on you.

Remember that forgiveness is a personal journey, and it might not happen overnight. Be patient with yourself and allow the healing process to unfold at its own pace.

WORKSHEET

Exercises

1. Describe a recent conflict you experienced and apply a conflict resolution technique discussed in this chapter.

Notes:

_____

_____

_____

2. Reflect on the role of forgiveness in conflict resolution. How does it facilitate healing?

Notes:

_____

_____

_____

3. Identify a key principle from the 'Art of Making Peace' section and explain how you can apply it in your daily interactions.

Notes:

_____

_____

_____

4. Analyze the conflict resolution techniques provided in this chapter. What techniques would you like to start applying?

Notes:

_____

_____

_____

5. Create your own scenario where forgiving strategies from the chapter could be effectively applied.

Notes:

_____

_____

_____

Practice Questions:

1. What are the key components of effective conflict resolution?

Notes:

_____

_____

_____

2. How can forgiveness impact the outcome of a conflict?

Notes:

_____

_____

_____

3. Discuss how empathy plays a role in resolving conflicts.

Notes:

_____

_____

_____

4. Describe a situation where poor conflict resolution led to negative outcomes.

Notes:

_____

_____

_____

5. Compare and contrast different conflict resolution techniques presented in this chapter.

Notes:

_____

_____

Key Takeaways:

1. Conflict resolution is an essential skill for maintaining harmonious relationships.

Notes:

_____

_____

_____

2. Forgiveness is not just beneficial for the aggrieved, but also for the overall resolution process.

Notes:

_____

_____

_____

3. Effective communication and empathy are critical in resolving conflicts.

Notes:

_____

_____

_____

4. Application of conflict resolution techniques can foster your relationship.

Notes:

_____

_____

_____

5. Understanding various conflict resolution techniques allows for a more adaptable approach in different situations.

Notes:

_____

_____

_____

Action Steps:

1. Practice active listening in your next conversation to enhance understanding and reduce potential conflicts.

Notes:

_____

_____

_____

2. Apply a conflict resolution technique in a real-life situation and observe the outcome.

Notes:

_____

_____

_____

3. Write a reflective journal entry on a past conflict and how it could have been resolved differently.

Notes:

_____

_____

_____

4. Discuss with a peer about their approach to conflict resolution and share insights.

Notes:

_____

_____

_____

5. Set a goal to proactively address conflicts in your personal or professional life.

Notes:

_____

_____

_____

Segue

In Chapter 4, "Addressing the Issues," we delved into the art of making peace. We explored conflict resolution, the grace of forgiveness, and the steps towards healing.

Conflict is inevitable, but it can catalyze growth and understanding when managed correctly. The trick lies in the approach.

Forgiveness is also touchy subject, especially when the wounds are fresh. But harboring resentment is like drinking poison and expecting the other person to die. Forgiveness doesn't mean forgetting, but it does mean releasing the burden of anger and bitterness. It's a gift you give yourself as much as you give your partner.

Now, as we turn the page to a new chapter, we embark on a journey from resolution to trust.

Chapter 5, titled "Trust and Transparency," shifts our focus to the foundation of all lasting relationships: trust. Trust is the bedrock upon which all strong connections are built.

As we transition from conflict resolution to trust-building, remember that trust is the outcome of resolved conflicts and healed wounds. It's a testament to the strength and resilience of human connections. So, let's turn this page with an open heart and a willing spirit, ready to embrace the lessons of trust and transparency. Together, let's build stronger, more trusting, and transparent relationships.

T - TRUST AND TRANSPARENCY

"Trust is the glue of life. It's the most essential ingredient in effective communication. It's the foundational principle that holds all relationships."

— STEPHEN COVEY

Trust is like a delicate porcelain figurine. Once it's broken, it can be fixed, but the cracks will always be visible. It's the bedrock upon which relationships stand, and without it, even the strongest bonds can crumble. This chapter will explore the importance of trust and transparency in relationships.

Trust should not be taken lightly. It's not merely a word we toss around. It's a commitment, a responsibility that we have towards our partners. And it's not just about being honest or loyal. Trust encompasses so much more. It's about being reliable, consistent, and living up to the promises we make.

Transparency, on the other hand, is about openness and honesty. It's about sharing your thoughts, feelings, fears, and dreams with your partner without fear of judgment. Transparency encourages open communication and discourages the buildup of resentment and misunderstandings.

Imagine a relationship where you can't trust your partner. Every word they say, every action they take, is questioned. You live in a constant state of anxiety and doubt. It's like walking on eggshells all the time. This is not a healthy or satisfying way to live.

Building trust and transparency in a relationship requires time, patience, and consistent effort. It's not something that happens overnight. It's a gradual process that involves open communication, understanding, and mutual respect.

To build trust, start with small actions. Be reliable. If you say you're going to do something, do it. If you make a promise, keep it. Consistency in your words and actions is the first step toward building trust.

Next, practice honesty. Be honest with your partner about your feelings, thoughts, and actions. This doesn't mean you must share every single thought that crosses your mind. But when it comes to important matters, honesty is crucial.

Transparency plays a big role in building trust. It's about being open and honest with your partner, sharing your thoughts and feelings, and encouraging them to do the same. Transparency creates a safe space where both partners can express themselves freely without fear of judgment or criticism.

Communicate openly about your expectations and boundaries. It's important to set clear expectations from the beginning of the relationship. This helps avoid misunderstandings and resentment down the line.

BUILDING TRUST

So, what is trust exactly? Trust is the confident expectation that someone will act in your best interest. It's the faith you place in them, the belief that they will be honest, reliable, and consistent. It's the assurance that they will keep their promises, meet their commitments, and uphold their responsibilities. Trust is about showing up, time and time again, proving through action that you are dependable.

Trust is not something that appears overnight. It's not a switch that can be turned on at will, nor is it a gift that can be handed over in a neatly wrapped package. It's an investment, a daily commitment, a steady accumulation of reliable actions and honest words. It must be earned, built over time, and nurtured with care.

Trust is a two-way street. It's a mutual exchange between two people. It's not just about trusting your partner but also about being trustworthy yourself.

Broadly, trust can be divided into two categories: Basic Trust and Emotional Trust.

Basic Trust is the initial layer of trust. It's the assurance that your partner will be where they say they'll be, do what they say they'll do. It's the type of trust that assures you that your partner will pay the bills, pick up the kids, or simply show up. Basic trust is procedural; it's the nuts and bolts.

Emotional Trust, on the other hand, is what you feel when you can share your innermost thoughts and feelings with your partner. You trust them to handle your vulnerability with care. Emotional trust is the one that takes the hit when there's betrayal. It's fragile, yet it's the most enriching type of trust.

Imagine you have a trust bank account with your partner. Every positive action, like keeping a promise or showing support, is a deposit. Every negative action, like lying or breaking a promise, is a withdrawal. Over time, these transactions create a balance that either fosters or degrades trust. The key is to keep making deposits, and the currency is consistency. That means being reliable not just once or twice, but always.

Building trust is a journey, a gradual process that takes time and effort. It's not a destination that can be reached overnight, but a path we should walk every day, showing the commitment to be consistent, honest, and reliable.

HOW TO KNOW IF YOU CAN TRUST EACH OTHER

Trust is the quiet certainty that your partner will respond to your needs and that they have your best interests at heart. But how can you tell if you and your partner have this level of trust? Let's explore this critical facet of relationships.

Firstly, a trustworthy person is *consistent*. They follow through with what they say and keep their promises. If your partner is reliable and their words match their actions, it's a good sign that they are trustworthy.

Secondly, *honesty* is a hallmark of trust. Being honest doesn't necessarily mean sharing every single thought or feeling, but it does mean being truthful about significant things. If your partner is open and truthful with you, even when it's uncomfortable, it suggests a high level of trust.

In addition to honesty, *transparency* is also key. This means not hiding aspects of one's life or feelings. If your partner is open about their feelings, their past, and their thoughts, it's a sign of trust.

Another critical factor is *respect for boundaries*. Everyone has certain limits and areas of privacy they wish to maintain. If your partner respects these boundaries and doesn't attempt to invade your personal space without consent, it shows they are trustworthy.

Trust also entails *emotional safety*. You should feel safe to express your emotions without fear of ridicule or dismissal. If your partner validates your feelings and listens to your concerns, it's a good indication of trust.

Of course, trust also involves a certain level of *vulnerability*. If your partner is comfortable being vulnerable with you and allows you to be vulnerable with them, it's a strong sign of trust.

Notably, trust evolves with time. It's built on a history of interactions and experiences. If your partner has proven over time that they can be relied upon, it's a clear sign of trust.

Trust requires *conflict resolution*. Disagreements are inevitable in any relationship. However, if you and your partner can navigate conflicts in a healthy way—by listening, understanding, and compromising—it indicates a robust level of trust.

Furthermore, trust involves *mutual respect*. If your partner values your opinions, listens to your ideas, and doesn't belittle you, it's a potent sign of trust. Respect shows that they take your thoughts and feelings seriously.

Lastly, trust incorporates a *sense of security*. You should feel safe—physically, emotionally, and mentally—in your relationship. If your partner provides this sense of security, it indicates a high level of trust.

REBUILDING TRUST: A PATH TOWARDS HEALING AND CONNECTION

"Trust takes years to build, seconds to break, and forever to repair." This quote resonates with many because it speaks to the fragility of trust. So, what happens when trust is broken in a relationship? You might feel like a ship lost at sea, unsure how to navigate the storm. But remember, even the biggest storm will pass, and the sun will shine again. It's about learning how to weather the storm and steer your ship back to the harbor of trust.

So, you messed up? Whether it's a small misstep like forgetting an anniversary or a major one like infidelity, rebuilding trust is a process that requires time, patience, and, above all, actionable change. What can pull you back is not necessarily grand gestures but consistent actions that demonstrated a commitment to change.

1. Acknowledge the Mistake: The first step in rebuilding trust is acknowledging the error. It's not just saying, "I messed up," but understanding how your actions impacted your partner.
2. Be Transparent: This is where you open the books. Be prepared to answer questions, even uncomfortable ones, as your partner seeks to understand the violation of trust.
3. Commit to Change: Saying "I'll never do it again" is not enough. You need to identify why you broke the trust in the first place and make concrete steps to change.
4. Be Consistent: Remember the trust bank account? Consistency is the key to making continuous deposits.

Rebuilding trust is not a simple fix. It's a process that requires patience, understanding, and commitment from both partners.

Rebuilding trust involves *forgiveness*. However, forgiveness is not about forgetting or excusing the behavior. It's about releasing the hurt and anger that holds you back. It's a personal journey that takes time and courage. Remember, forgiveness is for you, not the other person.

Equally important is the role of *empathy* in rebuilding trust. Empathy is about understanding and sharing your partner's feelings. It's about stepping into their shoes and seeing the world from their perspective. This emotional connection fosters trust and intimacy.

Rebuilding trust also requires *self-reflection*. It's about understanding your actions and their impact on your partner. This self-awareness is crucial for personal growth and change.

Maintaining trust requires a strong commitment to the relationship. It's about choosing your partner every day, even when things get tough. This commitment sends a powerful message of love and loyalty, strengthening trust.

THE POWER OF TRANSPARENCY

Transparency is a vital aspect of any relationship, particularly in romantic partnerships. It involves being open and honest with your partner about your thoughts, feelings, and actions.

Being transparent in a relationship means sharing your true self, including your dreams, fears, and past mistakes, however, transparency is not just about revealing your truth; it's also about being receptive to your partner's truth. It involves active listening and empathy, taking the time to understand their perspectives and feelings, and validating their experiences. It's about creating a safe and supportive space where both of you can express yourselves freely and honestly.

Transparency can enhance communication in a relationship. When you are open and honest, it encourages your partner to do the same, leading to better understanding and less miscommunication. It can also help prevent misunderstandings and conflicts, as issues are discussed openly and resolved before they escalate.

Transparency can also lead to personal growth. When you reveal your true self to your partner, it encourages self-awareness and introspection. It allows you to reflect on your thoughts, feelings, and actions, leading to personal growth and self-improvement. It also encourages your partner to do the same, leading to mutual growth and evolution as individuals and as a couple.

Transparency is also a way to show love and respect to your partner. It shows that you value their opinion, trust their judgment, and respect their feelings. It's a way to show that you care about their happiness and well-being, and are committed to building a healthy and fulfilling relationship together.

However, transparency is not about sharing every detail of your life or violating personal boundaries. It's about being open and honest about what matters in your relationship, respecting each other's privacy, and maintaining a balance between openness and personal space.

Transparency can be challenging. It requires courage to reveal your true self and vulnerability to open up to your partner. But the rewards are worth it. Transparency can lead to a more authentic, fulfilling, and resilient relationship, one that is built on trust, love, and mutual respect.

WORKSHEET

Exercises:

1. Identify an instance where you found it hard to trust your partner.

Notes:

_____

_____

_____

2. Reflect on a moment when transparency strengthened your relationship.

Notes:

_____

_____

_____

3. List actions you can take to rebuild trust after a breach.

Notes:

_____

_____

_____

4. Think about a time when a lack of transparency caused conflict in your relationship. How did you resolve it?

Notes:

_____

_____

_____

5. Consider ways in which you can be more transparent with your partner.

Notes:

_____

_____

_____

Practice Questions:

1. Do you feel you and your partner have established a foundation of trust in your relationship? Why or why not?

Notes:

_____

_____

_____

2.What are the indicators that suggest you can trust your partner?

Notes:

_____

_____

_____

3. How do you react when your trust is broken, and how do you expect your partner to react?

Notes:

_____

_____

_____

4. In what areas of your relationship do you think you and your partner could improve transparency?

Notes:

_____

_____

_____

5. Do you believe transparency can lead to a deeper connection and understanding in a relationship? Explain.

Notes:

_____

_____

_____

Key Takeaways:

1. Trust is the foundational block of any loving and lasting relationship.

Notes:

_____

_____

_____

2.Building and maintaining trust requires consistent and transparent actions and communications.

Notes:

_____

_____

_____

3. A breach in trust doesn't spell the end of a relationship; trust can be rebuilt with effort, understanding, and time.

Notes:

_____

_____

_____

4. Transparency in a relationship fosters trust, reduces misunderstandings, and promotes a deeper connection between partners.

Notes:

_____

_____

_____

5. Developing trust and maintaining transparency are ongoing processes that require mutual effort and commitment.

Notes:

_____

_____

_____

Action Steps:

1. Commit to being open and honest with your partner, even when it's uncomfortable.

Notes:

_____

_____

_____

2. Establish and respect boundaries, valuing your partner's privacy and expecting the same in return.

Notes:

_____

_____

_____

3. Communicate clearly and regularly about your feelings, expectations, and concerns to avoid misunderstandings.

Notes:

_____

_____

_____

4. Apologize and make amends when you break your partner's trust and work together to rebuild it.

Notes:

_____

_____

_____

5. Regularly assess the state of trust and transparency in your relationship and address any issues promptly.

Notes:

_____

_____

_____

Segue

So, you're here because you've navigated the seas of emotional intimacy and communication, two crucial cornerstones we've discussed in earlier chapters. Fantastic! But let's pause and acknowledge that no matter how intimate or communicative you are, your relationship will falter if you lack trust and transparency.

Trust is that invisible thread that weaves safety, security, and intimacy together. In many ways, it's the unspoken contract that assures both parties that they can be vulnerable, authentic, and respected.

In our hyper-connected world, where social media friendships can be mistaken for genuine relationships, transparency is the antidote to superficiality. It's what sets a deep, meaningful relationship apart from a casual one. Failure to be transparent can cost you dearly. It creates a breeding ground for mistrust and suspicion. Lack of transparency can manifest in different ways—financial secrets, emotional unavailability, or even just failing to share your daily experiences. In each case it erodes the relationship slowly but surely, often without either party realizing it until it's too late.

Trust and transparency are not isolated concepts but symbiotic. Transparency fosters trust, and trust fosters transparency. It's a virtuous cycle that feeds upon itself, making your relationship stronger and more resilient. It's the key to turning a good relationship into a great one. So, as you navigate the complexities of love and partnership, remember that the road to eternal happiness is paved with trust and transparency.

E- EVOLUTION OF INDIVIDUALS AND RELATIONSHIPS

"In the end, we only regret the chances we didn't take, relationships we were afraid to have, and the decisions we waited too long to make."

— LEWIS CARROLL

It's the beauty of life that we're not static beings. We change, grow, and evolve. This chapter delves into the fascinating dynamics of how individuals and relationships can evolve together, promoting mutual growth and fulfillment.

As we traverse the path of life, we undergo numerous changes and transformations. Our experiences shape us, our perspectives shift, and we find ourselves maturing and evolving over time. This ongoing evolution is essential to our personal growth and development. However, it's not just us who evolve - our relationships do, too.

Just like individuals, relationships are living entities. They breathe, grow, and evolve, reflecting the dynamic nature of human interaction. Our relationships adapt as we change and grow, mirroring our personal evolution. This continuous dance of growth and adaptation is what makes relationships rich, fulfilling, and profoundly meaningful.

One of the keys to a successful relationship is embracing this evolution.

This process of evolving together is not always smooth or straightforward. It requires patience, effort, and a deep understanding of each other. It's about recognizing and appreciating our individual growth while nurturing the growth of our relationship. It's about finding a balance between our personal evolution and the evolution of our relationship.

Evolving together also means learning to navigate the challenges and obstacles that come our way.

As we evolve together, we foster a deeper understanding and acceptance of each other. We learn to appreciate our differences, celebrate our similarities, and embrace our unique characteristics. We develop a profound respect for each other's individuality and a deep appreciation for the unique dynamics of our relationship.

Evolving together also involves fostering a shared vision and working towards common goals. It's about aligning our values, aspirations, and dreams and supporting each other in our journey towards these goals. As we work together towards our shared vision, we strengthen our bond and deepen our connection.

EVOLVING TOGETHER: NURTURING PERSONAL GROWTH AND RELATIONSHIP HEALTH

When we enter a relationship, we merge our lives with another person. But that doesn't mean we lose our individuality. We still have personal goals, interests, and a desire for self-improvement. And these individual aspects of our lives don't have to clash with our relationship needs. In fact, when managed well, they can contribute to a stronger, healthier relationship.

We often hear that opposites attract. But research shows that it's not the differences, but the similarities, that make for a lasting relationship. This doesn't mean we need to be identical to our partners. Rather, we should share core values, life goals, and a mutual understanding.

Yet, it's also crucial to respect and encourage each other's individuality. We should support our partner's personal goals and interests, even if they differ from our own. This will enhance our partner's personal growth and enrich our relationship.

But how do we encourage personal growth while nurturing our relationship? The key lies in communication, understanding, and compromise. We need to discuss our individual goals and interests with our partner and find ways to support each other in achieving them.

At the same time, we need to ensure that our individual pursuits don't undermine our relationship. We need to balance 'me' time and 'us' time, which can be challenging but necessary for a healthy relationship.

What if our personal goals seem to conflict with our relationship needs? In such cases, we need to reassess our priorities and make necessary adjustments. But we should never give up on our personal growth for the sake of our relationship. Remember, a healthy relationship involves two individuals growing together, not one person sacrificing their growth for the other.

A good relationship gives us the freedom to be ourselves, pursue our interests, and grow as individuals. It's a relationship that respects our individuality while fostering mutual growth. It's a relationship where we evolve together, not apart.

Research shows that couples who evolve together have healthier and longer-lasting relationships. They have a deeper understanding of each other, are more satisfied, and are more likely to overcome relationship challenges. So, let's strive to evolve together in our relationships.

INDIVIDUAL GROWTH AND ITS ROLE IN NURTURING HEALTHY RELATIONSHIPS

Personal development, the quest to become the best version of ourselves, is a topic that has gained significant attention in the past few years. It's a journey of self-discovery, exploring our potential, and expanding our capacities. Yet, as we explore our personal growth, we must not lose sight of its impact on our relationships, particularly romantic ones.

Personal growth is not a solitary pursuit. It influences and is influenced by our interactions with others, especially those we are closest to. A healthy relationship thrives on mutual growth and development. This growth not only strengthens the individual but also fortifies the bond between partners.

The importance of personal development in a relationship lies in its capacity to nurture two individuals within the shared space of 'togetherness'. It allows each person to flourish, grow, and evolve, while simultaneously strengthening the connection they share.

Investing in personal development means investing in the relationship. It paves the way for understanding, respect, and love to flourish. It keeps the relationship dynamic, preventing stagnation and promoting constant evolution.

But the question arises: How does one pursue personal growth in a relationship? The answer lies in finding and pursuing your own hobbies, passions, and interests.

Your hobbies and passions are an extension of who you are. They reflect your identity and contribute to your uniqueness. Pursuing them enriches your life and brings a fresh perspective to your relationship. It promotes understanding and respect for individuality, which are key elements of a healthy relationship.

Finding your passion may seem like a daunting task. But it doesn't have to be. Start with self-reflection. What activities make you lose track of time? What topics do you find yourself drawn to? What skills would you like to improve? These questions can lead you to your passions.

You become a happier person when you engage in activities that bring you joy and fulfillment. This positivity spills over into your relationships, enhancing mutual joy and satisfaction.

Once you've identified a hobby or passion, the next step is to pursue it. This might mean setting aside a specific time each week for your hobby, joining a club or group, or even taking classes to improve your skills. Cultivate patience and persistence, as mastery takes time. Remember, the goal is to enjoy the process, not just the outcome.

Pursuing your hobby is not a selfish act. When you give time to what you love, you refuel your emotional tank. You're also setting a positive example for your partner. You show them that it's okay to prioritize personal interests and that doing so can lead to increased happiness and fulfillment.

Hobbies can also serve as a form of self-care. They provide a break from the stresses and pressures of everyday life. They offer an outlet for creativity, a sense of achievement, and a chance to unwind. By prioritizing your hobbies, you're prioritizing your mental health.

Balancing individual growth with relationship growth can be challenging. Yet, it is essential. A relationship is a partnership, a union of two unique individuals. Each person brings their values, experiences, and passions to the relationship. These differences should not be seen as obstacles but as opportunities for growth.

RECOGNIZING AND UTILIZING YOUR STRENGTHS IN RELATIONSHIPS

Unearthing your unique strengths and putting them to use in your relationship is essential. You and your partner are separate individuals, each with your talents, abilities, and skills. Recognizing and leveraging these strengths can drastically improve the quality of your relationship.

Understanding your strengths begins with self-reflection. This isn't about ego or bragging about what you're good at. Instead, it's an honest assessment of your abilities, skills, knowledge, and talents. It's about owning what makes you unique and how you can contribute to your relationship in your special way.

For instance, if you're a good listener, you can use this strength to provide emotional support for your partner. If you're good at managing finances, you can take charge of the financial aspect of your relationship. This means using your strengths in ways that make your relationship stronger and more balanced.

It's also important to remember that strengths aren't static. They can grow and develop over time. For example, you might discover that you have a knack for cooking or gardening that you never knew about before. Embrace these newfound strengths and put them to use in your relationship.

In a relationship, it's important to balance the strengths of both partners. If one person's strengths are constantly overshadowed or ignored, this can lead to feelings of resentment or inadequacy. Both partners' strengths should be recognized and valued for your relationship to thrive.

Complementing each other's strengths is one of the keys to a successful relationship. For instance, if one partner is good at planning and the other is good at executing, they can work together to achieve shared goals. This synergy can create a stronger bond between the two of you.

It's also important to be patient with your partner's weaknesses. No one is perfect, and everyone has areas they can improve upon. Instead of criticizing or getting frustrated with your partner's shortcomings, try to find ways to support them. This might mean stepping in to help when they're struggling or offering words of encouragement when they're feeling down.

Understanding your strengths and how to use them in your relationship also involves communication. It would help if you expressed to your partner what you believe your strengths are and asked for their input as well. They might see strengths in you that you weren't even aware of.

Finally, always be open to learning and growing. Your strengths can always be enhanced, and you might discover new strengths over time. Keep an open mind and be willing to step out of your comfort zone. You never know what strengths you might uncover.

TIME TOGETHER VS TIME APART: THE POWER OF BALANCE

We all have different interests and hobbies. It's perfectly normal and acceptable to want to do different things. Sometimes, we can do activities together, and other times, we choose to spend some time apart. It doesn't signify a problem in our relationship, but rather, it's a sign of a healthy one.

The key to a successful relationship is finding the balance between time together and time apart. Spending every waking moment together can lead to feelings of suffocation and resentment. Conversely, spending too much time apart can cause feelings of neglect and disconnection. The goal is to strike a balance that promotes individual growth while nurturing the relationship.

The beauty of spending time apart is the opportunity it gives for personal growth. It allows us to pursue our individual passions, hobbies, and interests. This self-growth enriches us as individuals, which, in turn, enhances our relationships. We bring exciting new experiences, stories, and insights to share with our partners. This breathes fresh air into our relationships, keeping them vibrant and stimulating.

Spending time apart also fosters a sense of independence and self-confidence. We learn to be comfortable and content with ourselves, and this self-assuredness positively impacts our relationships. It reduces dependence on our partners for happiness and fulfillment, leading to healthier and more balanced relationships.

Now, let's not overlook the significance of spending quality time together. Shared experiences foster a strong emotional bond. They create beautiful memories that serve as the bedrock of the relationship. They deepen our understanding of each other and strengthen our emotional connection.

Time together also provides opportunities for meaningful communication. During these times, we can discuss our dreams, fears, goals, and concerns. Such discussions are crucial for maintaining a strong emotional bond. They ensure we're on the same page and moving in the same direction.

Scientific research supports the importance of both time together and time apart in relationships. A study published in the Journal of Marriage and Family found that couples who engaged in shared activities reported higher levels of relationship satisfaction. On the other hand, a study in the Journal of Social and Personal Relationships found that individuals who maintained their personal identities and independence in relationships reported higher relationship satisfaction. Both are equally important.

THE POWER OF SHARED GOALS IN RELATIONSHIPS

In life, we often find ourselves in relationships. We share our lives with others, be it a life partner, a close friend, or a family member. In every relationship, we have goals - things we hope to achieve together. Shared goals are not just about the big things, like buying a house or having kids. They can be about the small things too, like spending quality time each day or learning to cook a meal together.

Our shared goals give our relationships a sense of purpose. When we work towards common goals, we grow together. We face challenges, overcome obstacles, and celebrate achievements as a team. This shared journey strengthens our bond and deepens our connection.

However, creating shared goals can be challenging. It requires open and honest communication. We need to understand our own goals and desires first. Then, we need to share them with our partner and listen to their goals and desires. Together, we can create a vision for our future that reflects our shared values and aspirations.

Our shared vision serves as a guiding light in our relationship. It helps us navigate through the ups and downs of life. When we face difficulties, our shared vision reminds us of why we are together. It motivates us to overcome our problems and keep moving forward.

Research shows that couples with shared goals are more likely to stay together. They are more satisfied with their relationship and feel more connected to each other. Shared goals foster mutual understanding, support, and respect. They create a strong foundation for a lasting and fulfilling relationship.

Creating shared goals is not a one-time event. As we grow and change, our goals and desires may change too. We need to revisit our shared vision from time to time and adjust our goals and plans to reflect our changing needs and circumstances.

We learn a lot about each other in our journey towards our shared goals. We learn about our strengths and weaknesses, hopes and fears, dreams and ambitions. We learn to appreciate our differences and similarities and work together as a team.

Achieving our shared goals is not the end of our journey. It is a milestone in our ongoing relationship. Each achievement brings us closer to each other. It reaffirms our commitment and love for each other. It inspires us to set new goals and embark on new adventures together.

So, let's nurture our shared goals, communicate openly and honestly, support each other in our pursuits.

SETTING INDIVIDUAL GOALS IN RELATIONSHIPS

As we journey through life, goal setting is a powerful tool that can help us shape our future. In the context of a relationship, setting individual goals is just as important as setting shared ones. It's about growth, self-improvement, and remaining true to ourselves while being in a relationship.

Understanding your personal needs, desires, and ambitions is crucial to fostering a healthy and balanced relationship. Maintaining your individuality is essential, which includes following your own path, pursuing your interests, and fulfilling your unique goals.

Part of the beauty of being in a relationship is sharing your life with someone else. However, it's equally important to remember that you are still an individual with your own dreams and aspirations. Being in a relationship doesn't mean sacrificing your individual goals. Instead, it's about finding a balance between pursuing your personal ambitions and nurturing your relationship.

Honing in on your personal goals can help you maintain a sense of identity and self-worth. It allows you to grow as an individual, which in turn can enrich your relationship. You bring more to the table when you continuously learn, grow, and become your best version.

When you and your partner have personal goals, it can also foster mutual respect and understanding. It shows that you both value individuality and personal growth, which can deepen your connection and make your relationship more resilient.

While setting individual goals is important, it's equally crucial to communicate these goals to your partner. Open and honest communication about your ambitions can help avoid misunderstandings and potential conflicts. It allows your partner to understand your needs and desires and open a dialogue about how you can support each other in achieving your respective goals.

Remember, your individual goals shouldn't compete with your relationship goals. Instead, they should complement each other. It's about striking a balance between personal growth and relationship growth. So, while working on your personal goals, also remember to invest time and effort into nurturing your relationship.

Achieving personal goals can bring immense satisfaction and happiness. However, sharing these achievements with someone you love can make them even more meaningful. It can bring you closer, strengthen your bond, and create shared memories you can cherish together.

Setting and pursuing individual goals is a continuous process. It's not something you do once and then forget about. As you change and grow, your goals might also change. Regularly revisiting your personal goals can help you stay focused and motivated. It also provides an opportunity to celebrate your achievements and reflect on your growth.

SETTING RELATIONSHIP GOALS

Setting clear and shared goals with our partner is crucial in our journey toward a satisfying and enduring relationship. Goals give direction to our actions, bring us closer, and foster a shared sense of purpose.

Think about your relationship. What do you want to achieve together? Goals can range from simple daily habits to grand shared dreams. Maybe you want to improve communication, increase quality time, or plan a trip around the world.

Let's discuss a few practical goals that modern couples strive for to create a long-lasting relationship. Once you have that, your individual and mutual material goals will become so much more achievable.

- **Creating a Safe Emotional Space**: Building a safe emotional space is key. This means we can express our feelings, fears, and desires without fear of judgment or rejection. We should feel safe to be our authentic selves.
- **Improving Communication**: Aim to develop effective, open, and honest communication. This includes expressing feelings, discussing problems, and sharing joys. Active listening is also crucial.

- **Spending Quality Time Together:** In the hustle and bustle of life, spending quality time together often takes a back seat. Make it a goal to dedicate regular, distraction-free time for each other.
- **Maintaining Intimacy:** Physical and emotional intimacy is vital for a thriving partnership. From small gestures of affection to maintaining a satisfying sexual relationship, intimacy should be a priority.
- **Building a Strong Friendship:** A strong friendship forms the foundation of a long-lasting relationship. Cherish the friendship with your partner and nurture it.
- **Supporting Each Other's Goals:** Supporting each other's personal goals strengthens the bond. It shows respect for each other's individuality and encourages growth.
- **Practicing Honesty:** Honesty builds trust. It's essential to be honest, even when the truth is uncomfortable.
- **Practicing Forgiveness**: Mistakes and disagreements are inevitable. The ability to forgive and move on is a valuable goal.
- **Growing Together:** Aim to evolve together, adapting and growing through the ups and downs of life.
- **Planning a Shared Future:** Creating shared dreams and planning a future together can bring you closer. It's a testament to the faith you have in your relationship.

These are just examples. Your relationship goals could be different. The important thing is to reflect on what matters most to you and your partner.

Setting goals is just the first step. Achieving them requires effort, patience, and commitment. Remember that change takes time. Be patient with yourself and your partner.

Your relationship is unique. Celebrate that uniqueness. Tailor these goals to suit your relationship. Make them your own. After all, the journey is all about you and your partner.

As we move forward, let's keep these goals in mind. They will guide us in our quest for a fulfilling, enduring relationship.

DECIDING WHICH GOALS TO SHARE

When you think about your relationship, it's more than just shared experiences or mutual feelings. It's a partnership built on shared goals and dreams. It's about two people striving for a shared vision, supporting each other's aspirations while nurturing the bond between them.

In our busy lives, it's easy to forget to sit down and talk about our dreams, hopes, and plans. But this is essential for a lasting relationship. It's not enough to assume you're on the same page. You need to make sure of it.

The first step is to create a safe space to discuss your goals. This can be during a quiet dinner, a walk in the park, or while cuddling in bed. The key is to ensure that both of you feel comfortable and open to share your dreams and aspirations.

Next, try to listen more than you talk. Understand that your partner's dreams are as important as yours. Be supportive and show genuine interest. Ask questions and try to understand why these goals are important to them.

It's also important to discuss how these goals align with your shared vision. How do your individual goals fit into the bigger picture of your relationship? Are there any conflicts? If so, how can you resolve them? Remember, it's not about sacrificing your dreams for each other. It's about finding a way to make both work.

Once you've discussed your individual goals, it's time to talk about your shared goals. These can range from short-term goals like planning a vacation to long-term goals like buying a house or starting a family.

When setting shared goals, remember to be specific. Instead of saying, "We want to travel more," say, "We want to visit Italy next summer." This way, you can make concrete plans and take actionable steps toward achieving your goals.

While it's important to dream big, setting realistic goals is also crucial. Be honest about your capabilities and limitations. If a goal seems too daunting, break it down into smaller, manageable steps.

ACHIEVING GOALS TOGETHER

You might have heard the saying, "*If you want to go fast, go alone. If you want to go far, go together.*" In relationships, going together is the key. Let's discuss how you can set and achieve relationship goals as a couple. It's is important for sustaining and nurturing love that stands the test of time.

To start with, setting shared goals is about more than just having a common destination. It's about the journey you take together to reach that destination. This journey shapes your relationship, strengthens your bond, and brings you closer as a couple.

When you share a common goal, it fosters teamwork. You work together, support, and motivate each other to reach your goal. You celebrate your successes together and learn from your failures together. This shared experience deepens your connection and understanding of each other.

Setting relationship goals also encourages communication. You need to discuss your dreams, aspirations, and desires. You need to listen to your partner's thoughts, feelings, and ideas. This open and honest communication builds trust and rapport between you and your partner.

Working towards your goals together also teaches you how to handle challenges and solve problems together. You learn how to compromise, negotiate, and make joint decisions. These skills are invaluable in managing conflicts and disagreements in your relationship.

Moreover, achieving goals together boosts your self-esteem and your confidence in each other. It reinforces your belief in each other's abilities and strengths. It validates your efforts and hard work. This positive reinforcement strengthens your relationship and encourages you to set and achieve more goals together.

However, setting and achieving relationship goals is challenging. It requires commitment, patience, and perseverance. It requires understanding, respect, acceptance, love, trust, and faith.

But don't let these challenges deter you. Remember, every challenge you face together is an opportunity to grow together, to strengthen your bond and deepen your love.

WORKSHEET

Exercises:

1. Reflect on a situation where individual growth or change caused tension in your relationship.

Notes:

_____

_____

_____

2. Identify a personal interest or hobby you have embraced and shared with your partner.

Notes:

_____

_____

_____

3. List your strengths and consider how to utilize them to nurture your relationship.

Notes:

_____

_____

_____

4. Consider a shared goal you have with your partner and outline the steps to achieve it together.

Notes:

_____

_____

_____

5. Think about the balance between time spent together and time spent apart in your relationship. Is there room for improvement?

Notes:

_____

_____

_____

Practice Questions:

1. Do you and your partner have shared goals, and how do they contribute to your relationship's health?

Notes:

_____

_____

_____

2. How do you maintain your individuality and pursue your interests while being in a relationship?

Notes:

_____

_____

_____

3. In what ways do you and your partner support each other's personal growth and individual goals?

Notes:

_____

_____

_____

4. Do you believe that individual growth can enhance relationship health? Explain.

Notes:

_____

_____

_____

5. How do you find unity in your uniqueness with your partner, and how has it strengthened your relationship?

Notes:

_____

_____

_____

Key Takeaways:

1. Evolving together and nurturing personal growth are essential for maintaining a healthy and satisfying relationship.

Notes:

_____

_____

_____

2. Individual and relationship growth are interconnected, and one can significantly impact the other.

Notes:

_____

_____

_____

3. Maintaining individuality and pursuing personal interests enrich the individuals and the relationship.

Notes:

_____

_____

_____

4. Shared goals and values are the glue that binds partners together and enhances mutual understanding and respect.

Notes:

_____

_____

_____

5. Finding a balance between time spent together and time spent apart is crucial for maintaining individual identities and fostering relationship health.

Notes:

Action Steps:

1. Set individual and shared goals with your partner and create a plan to achieve them together.

Notes:

---

2. Encourage and support your partner in their pursuits and interests, and seek the same support for your pursuits.

Notes:

---

3. Regularly assess your relationship and make necessary adjustments to ensure both individual and relationship growth.

Notes:

_____

_____

_____

4. Maintain open communication about your individual growth and its impact on the relationship.

Notes:

_____

_____

_____

5. Strive for a balance in shared and individual activities to maintain unity and individuality in the relationship.

Notes:

_____

_____

_____

Segue

> *"Love doesn't make the world go round. Love is what makes the ride worthwhile."*

> — FRANKLIN P. JONES

The beauty of love is its power to endure, stand the test of time, and bloom in the face of adversity. However, a strategy is needed to reach the state of everlasting love and happiness in a relationship.

In a relationship, it's essential to understand that love is more than just a feeling. It is a commitment, a choice we make every single day. To love someone isn't about experiencing a constant state of romantic bliss. It involves accepting the good with the bad, the joys with the challenges, and the peaks with the valleys.

When we talk about a long-term strategy for love, we're looking at ways to keep that love vibrant and alive. This requires continuous work, effort, and commitment from both parties involved. But remember, it's not about striving for perfection. It's about creating a relationship that's real, with room for growth, understanding, and mutual respect.

LONG-TERM STRATEGIES FOR A LIFETIME OF LOVE

"To love someone long-term is to attend a thousand funerals of the people they used to be."

— HEIDI PRIEBE

This quote rings a bell. In a long-term relationship, you witness your partner change, evolve, and sometimes, you have to let go of the person they were. It's not an easy task, but it's a part of the journey we embrace when we commit to love someone.

Couples in healthy relationships have their ups and downs, but what keeps them strong is the commitment to keep the love alive. It's not a one-time event or a yearly anniversary celebration. It's a daily ritual, a daily choice.

Here are some common habits partners in such relationships develop over time to keep the bond strong and the fire burning:

- Every day, they say "I love you" to each other. It doesn't matter if they had a fight or are tired from work. Those three words are a daily reminder of their bond. They apologize when they hurt each other, even for the smallest things. It's not about fault or pride but about respect and care for each other's feelings.
- They prioritize their "us" time. They put away their phones, turn off the TV, and just spend time with each other. It can be over a simple dinner, a walk in the park, or lying in bed before sleep. Those moments of just being together, talking, laughing, or even sitting in silence are precious. They keep them connected and remind them that they are each other's priority no matter how busy their lives get.

Healthy relationships are also about how you handle disagreements, support each other's dreams, and grow together. They are about being partners in every sense of the word.

- When you disagree, try your best to listen to each other's point of view, not just hear the words but try to understand the emotions and thoughts behind them. You may not always agree, and that's okay. What matters is respecting each other's opinions and finding a compromise.

- Support each other's dreams and ambitions. Cheer each other on. Celebrate each other's successes and lift each other up during failures. Be each other's fan and critic.
- And as you journey through life, make sure to grow together. Learn from each other and from your experiences, evolve, not separately but together. You may not be the same people you were when you first met, and that's okay. Love and appreciate who you've become because you've grown together.

Long-term love is not a walk in the park. It's a journey with ups and downs, twists and turns. But it's a journey worth taking because at the end of the day, you have someone by your side who knows you, loves you, and chooses you, every single day. And that, my friend, is the beauty of a lifetime of love.

THE ART OF NURTURING RELATIONSHIPS: A STEP-BY-STEP GUIDE

"The ultimate test of a relationship is to disagree but to hold hands."

— ALEXANDRA PENNEY

Relationships, especially those of the romantic kind, can be challenging. Even the most resilient couples can face problems. But fret not! There are ways to cultivate a bond that will weather any storm.

Here's a step-by-step guide to help you foster and cultivate lasting connections:

Self-awareness:

- Understand your values, strengths, and areas for growth.
- Reflect on past relationships to identify patterns and lessons learned.
- Practice mindfulness in your interactions. Stay present and engaged in the moment.

Self-awareness is about understanding yourself, your desires, and your boundaries. It allows you to bring your best self into the relationship, contributing positively to the dynamic.

Respect:

- Respecting each other's opinions and emotions is crucial in healthy relationships
- A relationship based on respect serves as a positive model for others, including friends, family, and children.
- A respectful environment provides emotional safety, allowing individuals to express vulnerability without fear of judgment.

When we respect our partners, we acknowledge their feelings and thoughts, we listen without interrupting, and we express our own feelings and thoughts honestly and kindly. Respect also means understanding and upholding each other's boundaries.

Open Communication:

- Foster an environment of open and honest communication.
- Express your thoughts and feelings clearly and respectfully.

Talking and sharing dreams and ideas is crucial in a relationship. It encourages understanding and empathy. Taking time to talk about your day, thoughts, feelings, and dreams can bring you and your partner closer. It also helps in resolving misunderstandings and conflicts.

Empathy and Understanding:

- Put yourself in others' shoes to comprehend their emotions and viewpoints.
- Validate and acknowledge the feelings of those you interact with.

Workshops can also be an excellent tool for relationship improvement. These can range from communication and conflict resolution workshops to those focusing on intimacy and trust. Workshops often provide practical exercises and techniques that couples can apply daily.

Quality Time:

- Invest time in meaningful and fulfilling experiences..
- Create shared experiences to deepen the bond.

Stepping out of your comfort zone can bring growth and excitement. Trying new activities together, setting shared goals, or facing challenges as a team can strengthen your bond. It helps you see each other in new lights and creates shared memories.

Conflict Resolution:

- Approach conflicts with a problem-solving mindset.
- Seek resolutions that prioritize understanding and compromise.

Consider couples therapy. Therapy is not just for struggling couples; it can benefit couples seeking to deepen their connection. Couples therapy can reveal patterns, foster understanding, and offer solutions. It's a space where couples can express their feelings openly and honestly, fostering a closer bond.

Consistency:

- Be reliable and consistent in your actions and commitments.
- Demonstrate your dedication to the relationship over time.

Cultivating self-improvement in a relationship is an ongoing process. It requires effort, patience, and understanding. If you say you'll do something, do it. If you promise to be somewhere, be there.

Celebrate Successes:

- Acknowledge and celebrate achievements, both big and small.
- Share in the joy of each other's accomplishments.

Maintaining a sense of fun and playfulness is very important. Life can get monotonous, and it's easy to get caught up in the everyday grind. Taking time to celebrate, laugh together, can go a long way in ensuring the longevity of a relationship.

Gratitude:

- Express gratitude for the positive impact your partner has on your life.
- Regularly show appreciation for the unique qualities your partner brings to the relationship.

Expressing and practicing gratitude contributes significantly to the health and longevity of your relationships. Gratitude creates an optimistic and uplifting atmosphere to nourish and support a healthy environment for your relationships to thrive.

THE POWER OF RESILIENCE IN RELATIONSHIPS

Resilience is a crucial attribute for a thriving relationship. It's the ability to rebound from adversities or changes in the relationship. It's the capacity to adapt, to keep moving forward, even in the face of difficulties. Being resilient as a couple doesn't mean you won't experience hard times. It means you'll be better equipped to handle them when they come.

Resilience helps couples navigate the storms of life. It enables them to bounce back from setbacks or disappointments, turning each into a lesson rather than a defeat. Resilient couples are like bamboo in a storm—they bend but do not break. They have the strength to withstand the winds of change.

Research shows that couples who practice resilience are more likely to stay together and feel satisfied in their relationship. Resilience fosters trust, mutual understanding, and a sense of security within the relationship. It allows couples to maintain a positive perspective, even in the face of adversity.

However, building resilience in a relationship is a challenging task. It requires effort from both partners. To foster resilience, you must first understand each other's strengths and weaknesses. This understanding helps you both to lean on each other's strengths during challenging times.

Let's review the cornerstones of resilience building in a healthy relationship.

- Effective communication is key to building resilience. It involves expressing your thoughts and feelings openly and honestly, without fear of judgement. It also requires active listening—truly hearing, understanding, and responding to your partner's concerns.

- Another aspect of resilience is flexibility. Life is unpredictable, and change is inevitable. By being flexible, you can adapt to changes and challenges that come your way. It helps you to adjust your expectations and find solutions instead of dwelling on problems.
- Resilient couples also practice emotional regulation. They understand that it's okay to feel negative emotions. But they also know how to manage these feelings and not let them dictate their actions. They can step back, assess their emotions, and respond in a way that promotes the health of the relationship.
- Also, resilient couples know the value of caring for their mental health. They understand that their individual well-being impacts the relationship. Thus, they take steps to ensure they're emotionally, mentally, and physically healthy. They also encourage and support their partner in doing the same.
- Finally, resilient couples show appreciation for each other. They express gratitude for their partner, appreciating the small and big things they do. This act strengthens their bond and increases their resilience to face whatever comes their way.

WORKSHEET

Exercises:

1. Reflect on your long-term vision for your relationship. What does a happy, healthy future together look like to you?

Notes:

_____

_____

_____

2. Identify areas in your relationship where continual learning could lead to improved connection and understanding.

Notes:

_____

_____

_____

3. Think about a situation where resilience played a key role in overcoming relationship challenges.

Notes:

_____

_____

_____

4. Create a list of strategies you can adopt to nurture and strengthen your relationship over the long term.

Notes:

_____

_____

_____

5. Consider ways to integrate learning and growth into your relationship routine.

Notes:

_____

_____

_____

Practice Questions:

1. Do you and your partner have a shared vision for the future, and how do you plan to achieve it together?

Notes:

_____

_____

_____

2. How do you and your partner approach learning and growth within your relationship?

Notes:

_____

_____

_____

3. How can resilience enhance your relationship's longevity and satisfaction?

Notes:

_____

_____

_____

4. Do you have a plan in place to nurture and maintain your relationship over the long term? If so, what does it include?

Notes:

_____

_____

_____

5. How do you balance the pursuit of individual goals with the pursuit of shared goals and visions in your relationship?

Notes:

_____

_____

_____

Key Takeaways:

1. Long-term strategies and vision are essential for building a relationship that stands the test of time.

Notes:

_____

_____

_____

2. Continual learning and adaptation are crucial for nurturing and maintaining a thriving relationship.

Notes:

_____

_____

_____

3. Resilience enables couples to navigate challenges and emerge stronger, enriching the relationship's foundation.

Notes:

_____

_____

_____

4. Regular nurturing and intentional efforts are required to sustain love and happiness in long-term relationships.

Notes:

_____

_____

_____

5. Balancing individual and shared goals is essential for maintaining harmony and mutual growth in relationships.

Notes:

_____

_____

_____

Action Steps:

1. Develop a shared vision for the future with your partner and establish steps to achieve it together.

Notes:

_____

_____

_____

2. Commit to continual learning and adaptation to nurture the growth and development of your relationship.

Notes:

_____

_____

_____

3. Build resilience by learning from each experience to strengthen your bond.

Notes:

_____

_____

_____

4. Regularly invest time and effort in nurturing your relationship and keeping the connection alive.

Notes:

_____

_____

_____

5. Maintain a balance between individual aspirations and shared goals to ensure mutual happiness and fulfillment.

Notes:

_____

_____

_____

CONCLUSION

"The best and most beautiful things in the world cannot be seen or even touched—they must be felt with the heart."

— HELEN KELLER

In wrapping up, the essence of this book is not just about finding love or maintaining relationships. It's about nurturing a bond that can withstand the trials and tribulations of life, about growing together and fostering a deep and enduring connection.

We've explored the various facets of sustaining love and nurturing relationships through the "RELATE" framework. This framework is not just a set of guidelines but a way of living to help you and your partner create a loving, lasting, and meaningful relationship.

- *R*eflecting on your relationship is crucial. Self-awareness and an understanding of each other's needs, desires, and triggers are the foundation upon which a strong relationship is built. It's important to continuously assess the state of your relationship and work on the areas that need improvement.
- *E*ffective communication is a lifeline of any relationship. Learning to express yourself clearly and openly while also being a good listener can foster understanding and prevent misunderstandings. It's the key to resolving conflicts and building a stronger bond with your partner.
- *L*ove and intimacy are the heart of a relationship. Keeping the emotional connection strong and maintaining physical intimacy can keep the relationship vibrant and healthy. It's the small gestures of love and affection that make a big difference over time.
- *A*ddressing conflicts constructively is crucial. Every relationship faces challenges, and learning to deal with them in a healthy way can prevent lasting damage and promote growth. Forgiving and learning from past conflicts can strengthen your bond and deepen your understanding of each other.
- *T*rust and transparency are the cornerstones of a loving relationship. Being consistent, honest, and open can build a foundation of trust that can withstand the test of time. It creates a safe space where both partners can be themselves and share their thoughts and feelings without fear of judgment.

- Embracing personal growth and mutual evolution is essential. Supporting each other's growth and setting shared goals can lead to a fulfilling and balanced relationship. It's about evolving together and building a life that is meaningful and aligned with your shared values.

The workbook section is there to reinforce your understanding and help you put the "RELATE" framework into practice. It's designed to help you reflect, learn, and plan for the future of your relationship. Utilize it to track your progress and make conscious efforts to improve and strengthen your bond.

The best thing is that building a successful relationship is so rewarding. Every effort you put in brings you closer to a life filled with love, happiness, and fulfillment. The "RELATE" framework is not just a guide; it's a companion in your journey towards a healthier, more enduring, and deeply satisfying relationship.

So here it is, the sum of what this book is about, the essence of sustaining a loving, meaningful relationship with your significant other. It's your turn to embrace these principles and apply them in your life. May love, understanding, and happiness always light your path.

REFERENCES

Gottman, J. M., & Silver, N. (2015). *The Seven Principles for Making Marriage Work.* Harmony.

Hendrix, H., & Hunt, H. L. (2004). *Getting the Love You Want: A Guide for Couples.* Henry Holt and Company.

Chapman, G. (2015). *The 5 Love Languages: The Secret to Love that Lasts.* Northfield Publishing.

Perel, E. (2017). *The State of Affairs: Rethinking Infidelity.* Harper.

Johnson, S. M. (2008). *Hold Me Tight: Seven Conversations for a Lifetime of Love.* Little, Brown Spark.

Tatkin, S. (2016). *Wired for Love: How Understanding Your Partner's Brain and Attachment Style Can Help You Defuse Conflict and Build a Secure Relationship.* New Harbinger Publications.

Goleman, D. (2006). *Social Intelligence: The New Science of Human Relationships.* Bantam.

Schnarch, D. (2009). *Passionate Marriage: Keeping Love and Intimacy Alive in Committed Relationships.* W. W. Norton & Company.

Tannen, D. (2007). *You Just Don't Understand: Women and Men in Conversation.* William Morrow Paperbacks.

Gray, J. (2004). *Men Are from Mars, Women Are from Venus: The Classic Guide to Understanding the Opposite Sex.* Harper Paperbacks.

JOURNAL ARTICLES

Fincham, F. D., & Beach, S. R. (2010). Marriage in the new millennium: A decade in review. *Journal of Marriage and Family, 72*(3), 630-649.

Gottman, J. M., & Levenson, R. W. (1999). What predicts divorce? The relationship between marital processes and marital outcomes. *Journal of Personality and Social Psychology, 76*(5), 737.

Baumeister, R. F., & Leary, M. R. (1995). The need to belong: Desire for interpersonal attachments as a fundamental human motivation. *Psychological Bulletin, 117*(3), 497.

Hatfield, E., & Sprecher, S. (1986). Mirror, mirror: The importance of looks in everyday life. *Suny Press*.

Drigotas, S. M., Rusbult, C. E., Wieselquist, J., & Whitton, S. W. (1999). Close partner as sculptor of the ideal self: Behavioral affirmation and the Michelangelo phenomenon. *Journal of Personality and Social Psychology, 77*(2), 293.

Reis, H. T., & Shaver, P. (1988). Intimacy as an interpersonal process. *Handbook of personal relationships*, 367-389.

Aron, A., Melinat, E., Aron, E. N., Vallone, R. D., & Bator, R. J. (1997). The experimental generation of interpersonal closeness: A procedure and some preliminary findings. *Personality and Social Psychology Bulletin, 23*(4), 363-377.

Holmes, J. G., & Rempel, J. K. (1989). Trust in close relationships. *Close relationships*.

Gable, S. L., Reis, H. T., Impett, E. A., & Asher, E. R. (2004). What do you do when things go right? The intrapersonal and interpersonal benefits of sharing positive events. *Journal of Personality and Social Psychology, 87*(2), 228.

Bradbury, T. N., & Karney, B. R. (2004). Understanding and altering the longitudinal course of marriage. *Journal of Marriage and Family, 66*(4), 862-879.

WEB ARTICLES

"The Science of Relationships: What Makes Love Last?" by Susan Krauss Whitbourne, Ph.D. [Psychology Today].

"The Importance of Communication in Relationships" [Verywell Mind].

"10 Habits of Couples in Strong and Healthy Relationships" [HuffPost].

"The Role of Emotional Intimacy in a Relationship" by Sheri Stritof [Verywell Mind].

"Conflict Resolution Skills for Healthy Relationships" [HelpGuide].

"The Truth About Trust: How It Determines Success in Life, Love, Learning, and More" [Forbes].

"The Art of Active Listening in Your Relationship" [MindBodyGreen].

"Nonverbal Communication and Body Language in Relationships" [HelpGuide].

"The Power of Forgiveness in Relationships" [Psychology Today].

"How to Set Healthy Boundaries in Relationships" [Harvard Health Blog].

10 quotes to Inspire Active Listening in the workplace. (2023, August 10). English. https://www.roberthalf.com/us/en/insights/career-development/10-quotes-to-inspire-active-listening

٢